River Teeth Literary Nonfiction Prize

Series Editors:
Daniel Lehman, Ashland University
Joe Mackall, Ashland University

The *River Teeth* Literary Nonfiction Prize is awarded to the best work of literary nonfiction submitted to the annual contest sponsored by *River Teeth: A Journal of Literary Nonfiction*.

. . . . *The Untouched Minutes*

DONALD MORRILL

University of Nebraska Press : Lincoln and London

© 2004 by the Board of Regents of the University of Nebraska. All rights reserved. Manufactured in the United States of America ⊚

Library of Congress Cataloging-in-Publication Data
Morrill, Donald, 1955–
The untouched minutes / Donald Morrill.
p. cm. – (River teeth literary nonfiction prize)
includes bibliographical references (p.   ).
ISBN 0-8032-3238-1 (clothbound : alk. paper)
1. Morrill, Donald, 1955– 2. Victims of crimes –
Florida – Tampa. 3. Authors, American –
20th century – Biography. 4. English teachers –
United States – Biography. 5. Tampa (Fla.) –
Social conditions. I. Title. II. River teeth literary nonfiction prize (Series)
PS3563.08737 Z472 2004 362.88'092–dc22
2003017590

Those minutes had beggared Don, and so he needed to understand what that begging had been for. His life was part of it –
most vividly and elusively the life he had been allowed since that
afternoon. But as an answer, it was clearly insufficient.

Months later, a way to begin came to him.

> Dear Gregory:
>
> Today, I understand, in yet another way,
> why lights burn all night in certain upstairs
> bedrooms. I fathom anew what it means to be
> frightened by a towel or a tumbling seed. I'm
> reintroduced to the absurd sturdiness of a
> bubble, and the persistent hiding game of bro-
> ken glass and the timbre of its breaking. And
> so much else. And not enough else. I under-
> stand that these things result, partly, from
> begging you for my life, though I'm sure you
> don't remember that moment as Lisa and I do.
>
> Today is September 14, 2001. Tropical
> Storm Gabrielle (first known as Tropical De-
> pression 8) has come ashore near Sarasota,
> tossing the trees and throwing the blossoms.
> The rain caroms from the roof of the shed
> across the patio in jagged panes of spray, as
> though from the bridge of a ship. To watch the
> rain now plunging, veering sidewise, dashing
> at each new unsuspected angle is to feel al-
> most that the world is jutting upward, swoop-
> ing, jerking this way and that, buffeted, con-
> fused. And the trees' shimmying makes the

day appear as though everything is coming loose bit by bit.

Maybe it is. In New York, at "the pile" that was the World Trade Center until three days ago, the rescuers are casting away debris in buckets, still hoping for survivors, though it's raining there, too, bringing the dust to earth but now weighing everything down – more weight to the weight – and making it colder and slicker, and less likely that anyone trapped below the rubble can survive. On the radio, the reporters tell us about what they think they know, or what they believe it is responsible to tell us. Congress is giving the non-elected president money and sanction to go to war against terrorism, for the sake of future generations. The winds are gusting.

You, too, must be watching this storm and these broad events. We're being told by various pundits that we are New Yorkers, that the destruction on Tuesday wounded us, too. (Would they agree the reverse was true – that what transpired between you and me and Lisa makes New Yorkers into Tampans?) The war now seems obscure because the enemy is obscure, and the battleground far-flung and yet near. Many are shocked that the attackers in New York and Washington, and on the plane that was forced to crash in Pennsylvania, could have understood beforehand they would be killing themselves as well as so many innocent bystanders. Who wants to believe that humanity could offer such possibility? About this, you must have known better, even if you've never actually articulated it. You must have known for a long time that each of us holds the other's fate, most of all if he is willing to trade his fate for it.

So what is our correspondent begging for here?

• • • • • • • • • • •

On February 4, 2001, a Sunday, at 4 p.m., Don and Lisa lay dozing in bed when they were roused by a sound resembling the chime of a bud vase nudged from a shelf by one of their cats – except they no longer had indoor cats. Lisa stirred and peered down the hallway.

"Someone's breaking in!" she cried.

Don grabbed the phone and shouted "9! 1! 1!" as he punched the numbers madly over and over because the battery was low and the thing slow to respond. The intruder must have stepped back and then lunged through the door because there was a detonation, a shattering and brittle ripping, and with a few quick steps up the hallway – his nylon pant legs scuffing each other, his shoes clacking on the hardwood floor – he stood before the couple.

He – Gregory – was black, perhaps in his mid-twenties, broad, stuffed into a thickly padded jacket, and he wore no mask.

"Put the phone down," he said, and Don, naked, tossed it on the bed. "Get down," he said, and they crouched.

"I'm homeless," he announced, almost annoyed, "and I need money."

He asked if they had a gun. They said no.

3

"I don't have a gun," he declared. "But I have the means to strangle her if you resist."

Lisa, wearing only panties, tried to slip on Don's shirt that had been lying on the floor beside her.

"Take it off," he commanded, and she did.

. . . .

Lisa and Don live in a refurbished, coral-hued bungalow built in 1926, an early tract home now a "historic" house, as some people are wont to say, given the newness of most Florida structures. Their street adjoins one of the most fashionable old neighborhoods in Tampa, though their district is "in transition," given its motley of picturesque rehabs and new Spanish Med townhouses amid faded cinder block rentals and moldy hovels. Their street has been on the way up for several years. Ranch-style houses built in the forties and fifties have been torn down to make way for condos daubed with postmodern flair. Two blocks over, a playground for the new gentry – restaurants and bars, fashionable shops and luxury apartments – gleams at evening. Don and Lisa resent the increased traffic this transformation has invited but savor what it has meant for the property values. They had rented the house next door for seven years and were unable to buy until recently – in their mid-forties – thanks to the happy confluence of their moderate means and the grace of a neighbor who, selling out to retire to the beach, gave them a good deal. Coveted bungalows make up most of the block, but they are the only owners who live on it, they with their modest piece of the American dream. Nearly all their neighbors are younger professionals renting as they did, waiting for their deal.

When Gregory came down their alley and tore the lock off the gate of their privacy fence and crept across the cedar decking toward their back door, this was the neighborhood he'd been roaming, area 160 on the Tampa Police Department crime grid.

> At the back door (that vain French door Lisa and I both loved), after you had broken out a pane to verify that there would be no electronic alarm, you heard our shouts. You knew we were there. Yet you came on. You had decided. Could we call this determination "courage," "madness," "the deepest drug hunger"?
>
> The click-click of your heels on the hallway floor – how many times my own heels clicking there had pleased me.
>
> The wired loneliness in the paused air as we seemed to wait for you to come through the bedroom doorway. Three seconds, at most.
>
> You were about to enter the room. You knew we were there. That's why we thought you had come to kill us.

. . . , ...

There was at least one other reason such a thought might have occurred to them – though, for all its vividness, it would have been obscure at that moment. Earlier the same week, Half and Susanne Zantop, professors at Dartmouth, were stabbed to death in their home in New Hampshire. Despite Lisa and Don's initial revulsion at this sensational crime – accompanied by a grim identification with the victims (with whom they shared the same occupation) – their attention, like that of most of the country, was soon redirected by personal and professional obligations. In their case, this involved an unusually demanding round of appointments at the office and the hosting of house guests, a couple (old friends) and their small son. Two nights before, the boy had blown bubbles from a plastic pipe Lisa had bought for him. The house had glistened as those rainbowed globes bobbed and crashed. Later, after everyone else had gone to bed, his father and Don had sipped their whiskies and remarked on how several bubbles had come to rest intact on the floor and lamp stand in the dining room. They'd wondered, with calm disinterest, how long the bubbles would survive the foot traffic, even the movement of air.

According to one of the news reports – which Don can still barely bring himself to read, though they pile up on his desk – "Half Zantop had defensive wounds on his hand and died from a stab wound to the heart even before his throat was cut. Susanne Zantop was stabbed in the right side of her head and face, and her throat was slit, apparently from behind."

• • • • • • • • • • •

Gregory stood at one corner at the foot of the bed, Lisa and Don kneeling side by side at the other. Don's head sank – an involuntary gesture of mourning for what was about to happen, for the absurdity of dying this way. He saw with astonishment – with absurd coherence – that they were going to die and that it seemed preposterous, and yet this is the way these things happened. The astonishment that pressed down on him, he later realized, surely must have visited those others whom we come to know, fleetingly and yet repeatedly, from the headlines of murder stories. No one thinks he is among the chosen – like those in the plunging airliner or the sinking ship, introduced, briefly, to their new status. . . .

After the astonishment, he went slack – the capitulation of snagged prey about to be devoured – then terror returned.

6

His hands flapped. Though she didn't mention it to Don until months later, Lisa remembers Gregory standing directly over him. Don was calling him "sir" and asking him to take whatever he wanted.

· · · · · · · · · · ·

For at least a couple of years before that afternoon, worry used to wake me in the night. I had come to a point in my life (midlife?) where I would lie in the darkness imagining the roots of the ancient cherry laurel beside our house cracking the foundation, breaking the sewer main. I'd revisit what I'd said in a meeting at the office the day before, suddenly certain I'd mishandled the matter. I'd cringe at the stock purchase I'd made, or hadn't made, months before. I'd lie embarrassed to simply be alive, acting as I act, having the job I have and so on. My pathetic life . . . and I too cowardly to describe myself as I really was. (It all seemed unworthy of what I'd once assumed I was and what I would become.)

Also, on occasion, I would be confronted by the vision of coming home to find Lisa dead or murdered . . . or of picking up the phone to find she had been in an accident. When she rolled out of the driveway in the morning, I would sometimes call to her, "Be careful!" echoing the ferociously anxious aunties of my adolescence.

Worse, in moments of stillness – while lying in bed or driving down the interstate or

7

sitting in a meeting of the committee on frit-
tering – scenes of violence would rise into me,
as if to assert again the vulnerability of each
thing and demand a wince at the chaos loaded
into every plan.

Why such dread? Stress at work? Exhaus-
tion of a hectic social life? A lifetime of grisly
headlines? Perversity of my nature? A furtive
form of self-regard? Or is it that one cannot
elude certain conclusions after enough mortal
illnesses among friends and family, enough
catastrophes borne on the ordinary?

Most people, I believe, would describe
me as easy-going, a happy man. I would have
added: lucky.

• • • • • • • • • •

Crouching beside Don, Lisa saw Gregory glance toward the bed.
She could also see that Don, with his head down, absorbed by his
terror, had left her alone.

Six months later, she acknowledged to him that she realized
then she had to watch out for herself, though what kind of vig-
ilance that might require was unclear. She imagined Gregory
knifing Don. She imagined Gregory forcing her to suck his cock.
She imagined him taking her to an ATM, emptying her account,
and then compelling her to drive to the dead end of a remote
road.

Later still, she recalled that as Don had tried to contact 911
and the back door had exploded, the urge to crawl under the bed
had swept through her, though not even a small child could find
room enough to hide there.

Several months after that, she remembered thinking that she might hide in the closet but had not done so because it didn't seem fair to Don: "This was happening to both of us, and I had to face it, too. I also thought Gregory would be angrier and more violent if he knew I was there, trying to elude him. I had no hope I could be more knowing. His assumption of power took that away, even my knowledge of our own house."

Lisa had rarely, if ever, been afraid at home. As a girl, she had been the little sister who'd volunteer to discover for her older siblings the source of the noise in the downstairs darkness. As an adult, she had lived alone in several cities, and she felt no qualms about being on her own when Don was out of town. She'd never had an interest in "getting a rush from horror," in haunting her imagination that way, as it seemed to her many people did, and so she often refused to view what she considered gratuitously brutal imagery, declining to see a new movie, for instance, if advised that it was particularly violent. Partly to that end, she and Don didn't keep a television in the house.

· · · · · · · · · · ·

Of course, you can hardly care about that, or anything else in these fragments I seem to be writing to you – if I am writing to you at all, here in some sort of tropical depression of my own.

"I don't want to hear about him anymore," Lisa says today. "I don't want to think about it. You, it seems, want to make something beautiful out of something ugly."

I stifle my reply, though I do wonder why any writer would want to make something

9

beautiful out of something already beautiful.

I suppose I would like to make out of what occurred between us something that is just. But that's much more difficult. Perhaps it's impossible, for all the claims of literature.

"You act as though nothing bad ever happened to you before," Lisa says.

She doesn't say (though I believe she thinks it): "You seem to be treating this as some great opportunity."

She's partly right. But am I wrong for that?

She's not beyond invention herself. After all, she named you less than a week after you busted in on us – named you without provocation as we drove down the interstate, again tearing at the details of you. (Gregory, she announced, is the name by which your family, but no one in your street life, knows you – since you've concocted a thug handle to fit your criminal persona). She also gave you a mother who is ill and yet still "believing in you," still asserting that you'll at last give up your mighty pleasure in flashing a roll of bills for your friends and breaking heads, that you'll take a regular job and settle down as you were taught to do.

Lisa was playing with her disturbance about our encounter with you, seeking some command over it. She – a writer, too – needed to tell the story of what came before and after that day with you, since neither of us believes you'll be caught. She needed to make you into someone other than a stranger in our bedroom. That's why she decided you permanently injured your shoulder when you crashed through our door, and why she later said you were blown away by the owner of the next house you invaded. The day she named you she wanted me to play along, but I wasn't up to it. In passing, months afterward, she told me she regrets her inspiration since now we mention you as though we know you.

I've often preached to my writing students, "Experience doesn't matter just because it happens to you," or, "Your experience is of interest because it is experience, not because it is your experience."

But experience is unique, since all actions are incommensurate, despite their effects, and their beginnings and endings are obscure. You can never know another's bliss, or sorrow. You can never know the other side of the eye. By definition, all experience is the experience of a survivor: experience must be survived in order to become experience. After all, could you really call being murdered an experience?

I seem to want to break you into a hundred reflections (like the broken glass of our back door), and I want to break those minutes into a hundred other experiences, as

though that time and our actions were not
only ours in themselves, or not only themselves. Do I want more survival?

I certainly want revenge, though there is
no revenge, no eye for an eye because of what
each eye has seen. Revenge craves an approv-
ing god. But there is only the inspiration of
further consequences.

And maybe this writing is some kind of
punishment, no longer even autobiography
transformed by meditation. No one is safe
from another's hands, or his own.

You surely have to laugh at me, you
motherfucker.

• • • • • • • • • • •

Though *home invasion* is listed among the offenses in Lisa and
Don's police department incident report (#01-009041), it does
not appear as a category among the crime statistics on the Tampa Police Department Web site, nor on the Web sites of the U.S.
Department of Justice or the National Criminal Justice Research
Service. According to these agencies, and others in the United
States, Don and Lisa were experiencing a burglary or robbery, for
that is how such crimes have been counted – unless an episode
has resulted in greater violence.

According to the Canadian Centre for Justice Statistics – currently one of the few organizations trying to gather such information on home invasions – part of the problem is the indefinite
nature of the crime as it unfolds. It often begins with a forcible
and spectacular entry by an assailant who knows the victim is
home (though some assailants enter by pretense or imperson-
ation). But, given the circumstances and the people involved,

things can go any number of ways thereafter. As a criminologist colleague told Don, "These people don't carry a union card that says *I only rob banks* or *I only steal cars*. They multitask. They want the money or the TV or the jewelry, sure, but if they get somebody cornered, under their control, they can take advantage of the situation. These are crimes of opportunity. You're lucky. This could have been a murder-rape-murder."

Because a uniform description of home invasion doesn't yet exist, there are no reliable figures. But the Canadian Centre, drawing on reports from Canada between 1995 and 2000, offers two counts – one based on a "narrow" definition, which involves "only incidents where the police have reported a robbery in a private residence," and a "broad" definition, which "includes robberies of a residence as well as any residential break and enter incidents where there is a violent offence." The former count puts the incidence rate at 9 to 11.5 per 100,000 population; the latter, at 23 per 100,000.

How many of the 443 burglaries in Tampa in February 2001 were actually face-to-face encounters? The Tampa Police understand the difference, even if they are not counting the distinction. One attending officer told Don and Lisa that their experience was "anomalous." Usually, the officer said, the invader comes around midnight or just before dawn. But a report on home invasions by James T. Hurley of the Fort Lauderdale Police Department suggests that they occur at all hours. It further asserts that the earliest victims of this crime, in the late 1970s and early 1980s, were the elderly and the "cocaine cowboys" of South Florida. Now, however, citizens of all kinds have become attractive targets, especially since convenience stores and gas stations – the traditional focus for robbery – have fortified themselves so well in recent years.

13

Few of Don and Lisa's friends and acquaintances seem to know the term *home invasion*. (For a while, Don wondered if it was merely an ephemeral invention of the sensationalist press.)

"You mean you were *there* when the guy came in?" people ask, astonished.

Yet some then offer an echoing story: the next-door neighbor axed; the robbers not entering the infant daughter's room but choosing the room opposite it, for no apparent reason; the rapist appearing out of the darkness beside the porch, placing a thumb over the woman's eye and whispering, "Scream and you lose it."

And these tales proffer commiseration of a sort. They insist that we are not alone – though the most vivid moments of memory both conjure and invade solitude.

Lisa and Don were not actually burglarized. No one "went through" their things. No one tried on their shoes and tossed them aside in disdain. No strew of papers and underwear. No piss left on the dining room table to taunt them, no turds bragging on the windowsill.

And there are no statistics for traumatized imaginations – for the aftermath.

As Don might say, though he will probably never get the chance, any discussion like this is really just another episode in our hopeless waking up.

• • • • • • • • • •

In that aftermath, with a peculiar frequency, people asked Lisa and Don, "Why do you think he chose you?"

Don imagines that beneath this concern lies the hope – which most would repudiate if it were made public – that perhaps he and Lisa deserved the invasion: the victim, because he is the victim, incites his victimhood.

"Yeah," Lisa sighed one day, disgusted with the idea. "They want to think that they're smarter somehow than we are, and so they're safer."

Shortly after the Zantops were murdered, the press pondered the motives for the killings. The stack of early news stories on Don's desk still asks: Was it a robbery gone wrong? A thrill kill, despite so much apparent rage? Was it related somehow to the fact that the Zantops were naturalized citizens originally from Germany? (They were murdered on the same date as Holocaust Remembrance Day in that country.) Perhaps they knew their assailants?

Briefly, around the initial expressions of grief and stunned sorrow, around the eulogies, lingered the faint consideration – an ancient ringing – that the killed might be implicated in their deaths, perhaps because their deaths were so horrible.

• • • • • • • • • • •

I'm slow-witted. I make personal what is merely human, ubiquitous, numeric, perhaps as formal as a socioeconomic model, or as obdurate as a particular gob of DNA surviving into the next generation. I make intimate what is unintended for me as I am, or even as I believe I am.

And yet, if face-to-face isn't personal, what is it?

I think you can understand me. After all, you said you had "the means" to strangle Lisa. You had more than homie-speak, more than street slur. I believe you're educated. You were quite the rhetorician, quite the sophist.

15

"I'm homeless, and I need money."

Perfect. Invoking this social wrong, assigning it to us, and then demanding restitution. Absurd, this notion of guilt, even though everyone is culpable, really; most accusations are just inappropriately timed.

"Many crimes are political acts," one of my friends claims. "We merely choose not to see them as political acts."

We wondered for a while if maybe you hadn't committed a worse crime in the neighborhood and simply needed our car to get out fast. Or maybe you'd entered the wrong house? (Who would you have been after at that hour among our neighbors?)

Experts assert that a person is more likely to be murdered by someone he or she knows than a stranger, but this can only be true in a world of the narrowest definitions. Those who vanished in the WTC, for instance, were killed by strangers who thought they knew their victims well enough to decide their fate, and strangers have been deciding such things, with varying degrees of directness, in vast numbers for millennia.

I remember that report from the Fort Lauderdale Police: "Home invaders usually target the resident, not the residence."

So who were we to you? Easy? Deserving?

"He had no interest in us," Lisa said of you, trying to erase one ambiguity.

• • • • • • • • • • •

What had Gregory decided when he glanced at the bed? Had he decided anything at all?

The bed was new, unlike the rest of the mission-style furniture in the house, items gathered during Don and Lisa's wanderings or through Don's brother, an antique dealer and their agent for tasteful pieces purchased on a budget. It was larger than the previous bed, so for some time, habituated to the former proportions of their domestic space, Don and Lisa had bruised their thighs on its edges in the dark. Of course, Gregory couldn't have known this, among the things he might have known about them. Nor could he have known that the small lacquered boxes on the bookshelves were Don's souvenirs of Burma. Or that the battered Scan Design dresser was one of the last remaining objects in the house from Lisa's first marriage. He couldn't have known how often Don had complained about Lisa's clothes hanging on the doorknobs around them, or how Don had finally given up on breaking her of this habit by joking that he would make her a clothes rack studded with a dozen doorknobs instead of pegs.

Lisa and Don had not been making love when they heard that first chime of broken glass – though fifteen months later Don sometimes allows the inference to be drawn when he tells of that afternoon, since it flatters his anxious hopes for plentiful desire in his marriage and also heightens the violation in question. (As though what occurred was somehow not violation enough.) Lisa and Don had, in fact, offered themselves to lovemaking, but they were too tired. There had been the house guests, of course, who had departed that morning. But Lisa had also just returned from the airport, where she had picked up another in the lengthy train of candidates for a professorship in their department – another whom they would interview at dinner, that evening. The engagement, while important to the advancement of university business, would proceed through familiar questions and answers, diverging at intervals for repeated or anticipated anecdotes – while permitting, Don fancied, brief, individual escapes from the dullness via sips of better white wine that shook the palate with summer lights and the dream of free hours in which one lived truly.

Lying in their new bed, Don had considered going to the health club nearby, to jar himself into readiness for the forthcoming duties. Had Gregory arrived a half hour later, he might have found Lisa alone. A half hour earlier, he would have found Don alone. Lisa and Don still occasionally contemplate these possibilities. They try to imagine the difficulties for the one laboring to relate what had happened and for the one bewildered in comforting the other – had there been an other left to comfort. In such moments, they soon agree with the utmost sincerity, that they are fortunate to have suffered that afternoon together, and to be left with their shortcomings.

Gregory looked at the bed, and Don now can't let himself imagine what Lisa really thinks of him, or the intruder, in the singular 4 p.m. where she kneels alone.

• • • • • • • • • •

Do you recall the man some years ago who leapt into the Potomac to save some of the hapless passengers in an airliner that had plunged into its frigid, winter waters – the man who saved some strangers but drowned?

What would you be willing to do for the other?

In your bedroom, for instance, would you lunge between that person and the assailant's knife strike?

18

What would you do for yourself?

Don't hurry to answer.

It's not clear how likely, even in the most extreme circumstances, you, or anyone, might be allowed a choice. For months, Don wondered, as no doubt many did, about the Zantops' final minutes. Apparently, Half Zantop was murdered first, and, given the evidence revealed by the press, he may have been surprised by his attacker.

One of Don's friends spent great energy telling him that he had done all the right things that afternoon. (So, apparently, Don seems to her a man who would be devastated by his apparent powerlessness to fend off an intruder.) She was trying to comfort him, and for this he is grateful, but. . . .

Another friend concluded, with a chuckle at the truth of her wayward expression, "You could live with being dead easier than not having done what might have helped someone not be killed."

• • • • • • • • • • •

Maybe, having burst through our door, you
now lead somewhere crucial – and that's why
I'm unable, so far, to follow you.

You're my invader, and I make you precious
to me. Isn't that corrupt?

Or am I corrupting you – trying to capture
you? So slight, you are, compared to the sufferings and longings of the world.

And you're not mine but Lisa's, too. You're
everyone's invader.

Are you some proof?

The roots of the old cherry laurel outside

19

the bedroom window have been edging under the foundation of this house for decades, seeking water, the slightest hint of steady nourishment. The slowest seepage from an underground pipe can invite the wormy inveigling of its furthermost tips. And they can break a house.

There's something in that relationship – house and tree, bough shade and easy chair – that resembles this correspondence. You're breaking in on me, over and over. You don't know where you lead or where you lead me.

Maybe you're a passage thrust upon me. Maybe a passage moves out through you – back down the hallway of this house, beyond that French door not yet exploded and through which a late afternoon sun I have often admired spreads a mat of light on the scarred and dusty hardwood floor.

· · · · · · · · · · ·

Three days after the Zantops were killed, their local paper, the *Valley News*, ran a story with the headline, "Victims Committed To Social Issues":

Half and Susanne Zantop made the ivory tower of academe a place for hard questions, harder answers and plenty of laughter, colleagues said yesterday.

"She was not one who looked for facile answers," said Gerd Gemunden, a Dartmouth Professor of German studies who worked with Susanne.

Half, 62, taught earth science and specialized in economic geology, the study of the formation and value of ore deposits. Susanne, 55, who chaired the German Studies Department, specialized in 18th- and 19th-century German literature.

But for friends, those brief autobiographical descriptions repeated in media accounts of the couple's Saturday deaths aren't enough for a couple with a broad range of interests, a couple with the ability to balance the pace of academic life with family and friends, and a couple that could be counted on for anything from a home-cooked meal to shelter for those with nowhere else to go.

In the introduction of her 1997 book, *Colonial Fantasies*, an examination of the relationship of the colonial idea and the German national identity, Susanne described her personal journey, first as a political science student in Berlin who "cheered the Chinese Cultural Revolution as the end to all bureaucratic ossification."

From there, she wrote, she and Half, by then a geologist with U.S. mining companies based in Latin America, "were living comfortably off salaries provided by American companies in Costa Rica" while demonstrating against the United Fruit Co. And, later, she found herself "siding with the 'oppressed' in the safe haven of New England academe."

It was, she said, "the trajectory from a self-satisfied anti-imperialist '60s radical to a guilt-ridden reluctant participant in U.S. imperialism to a critic of imperialism and my own involvement in it."

... Susanna and Half were committed to social issues, friends say. One of their main reasons to become U.S. citizens about three years ago was so they could vote, said Irene Kacandes, a professor of German studies and comparative literature.

"As any postwar German, she (Susanna) was sensitive to politics in people's lives," said Bruce Duncan, a Dartmouth professor of German studies.

Half, Kacandes said, often used his sense of humor when he was talking about politics or social issues. "He could get you out of an entrenched position by making you laugh," she said. . . .

．．．．．．．．．．．

Two weeks after kneeling in the bedroom, Don turned to Lisa and said, "You know, the funeral would have taken place by now."

This proposition made them stare at the living room around them, the minutes stretching to the gauge of gossamer but retaining the sturdiness of piano wire. Lisa and Don sat silent, listening, perhaps, for whatever eulogies nested in their possessions.

The night after the invasion, they stayed with friends. Lisa, rigorously placid, held Don, racked with alertness, almost till dawn. But the next afternoon Don returned to the house alone. (Lisa could not yet bring herself to approach it.) He eased open the kitchen door but paused on the porch in the sunlight, telling himself that this, too, was ownership. The interior before him seemed dark, abandoned, colder than the outside air. Occasionally in the past, he had encountered the odd unease of entering a dwelling after even a few days' absence: the odorless suggestion that something unverifiable had occurred in the rooms empty of people, the rooms as nonnegotiable as creature sleep. In those instances, he strode into the house and switched on lights, threw open windows, all to violate the immured time there and dispel it.

Now he stepped through the doorway. One step. Then another. He peered around each corner as though he might find Gregory there waiting for him – as though he would know what to do then! The injured doorway appeared doubly darkened by a home-made plywood dolly that he and his next-door neighbor had nailed over it the evening before. The dolly had lain rotting for years in the garage next door, and Don – during the years he had rented that house – had vowed to transport it to the dump. He had hauled it as far as the trash pile in the alley before buying the current house, and his next-door neighbor had taken the dolly no farther. As the evening dimmed on the wreckage of the afternoon, he and the next-door neighbor – who stumbled after Don with a precarious solicitude – searched for something to tack over the entryway and discovered the dolly. It fit perfectly, though rot and termite damage frayed its edges. A red, spray-painted X faced Don now – another simple ironic sign – and he thought of the rusted wheels on the other side of it. We believe we understand our relationship to objects, but then events cast a thing into an unexpected location, or assign to it a task unimagined by its designer, and we must guess again about character and fate. Don had known that dolly ten years – a rig left behind, he'd assumed, by a previous renter, perhaps its maker. Don had dragged it around the garage, out of the way, until he had decided it must go to the dump, to be churned into the land. Yet here it was, as though it had been anticipating this moment of transformation.

He crept down the hall, hearing his shoes clack on the hardwood. He peered into each room. His study, with the books and papers on his desk as they were the day before, disturbingly still. Lisa's bathroom, smelling oddly of fresh soap but cold and dim.

He jumped at the *thunk* of a cherry laurel seed falling on the back deck – because, it became clear to him in the succeeding weeks, Gregory must surely be coming back to kill them, to finish the job.

He paused where Gregory had stood over him at the foot of

the bed. While stripping the bed and remaking it, hurriedly, with fresh linen, he discovered a black sole mark on the floor where Gregory had stood over him. He touched it, to know it was there. Then he rubbed it away.

．．．．．．．．．．．

Take whatever you want, I said. Well, almost anything. It's a truism that things don't really matter and that we discover this at the moment of greatest danger.

Things matter because we do so much for them. That we could forsake them all to save ourselves only measures the importance of the threat to our lives. At that moment of utmost unpossessiveness, one, in fact, makes his life into a thing to be possessed, the ultimate possession for which all other property rights are traded away (in the implied business deal, as though that deal were a universal, automatically understood by everyone).

Usually, we don't think of a life as a thing, though we treat parts of our lives as a commodity. We "spend" time and convert it into other things with our labor. We think, too, of life as a tenuous possession. We say life can be "taken away" from us at any instant – as though we would then still exist somewhere but without our former status.

Taken away. Something in that expression (as in the expression "giving your life") simplifies our condition and obscures our connection to everything around us (which must also be part of our life). So where does the property of our living, or our dying, end?

Years ago, when I was first traveling around Asia and discovering the world for and in myself, I would walk the streets for hours day and night, for months. And because I was at a time of going forth, no matter how much I tossed the dust of irony on each thing I encountered, each thing gleamed.

Sometimes the gleam would fill me. I felt as though I were a cell, or bubble, taking in more and more of that liquid light.

And when I grew sated, the filling didn't stop. It seemed to press exhausted tears from me – as it does now – but they didn't reduce the pressure of experience. I felt as if something in me would burst, and I didn't know if this would be an end or a beginning.

A week after you came, I found two of the soap bubbles my friend's son had blown still serenely intact – one on the lamp table in the dining room and one on the floor beside the cedar chest.

. . . .

In the bedroom, after he had established the situation, Gregory drew a long breath, like a minor functionary trying to calm himself before making his first public speech.

Don is still thankful for the composure that breath seems to have confirmed in Gregory, though at the time this poise only conjured a more terrifying ambiguity. Was this intruder hoping merely to reassure them, to disarm them further?

Gregory then pulled from his back pocket a navy blue and white bandana knotted at the corners. He slipped it onto his head, adjusting it carefully. Don wondered if it might not be his gang rack. Maybe this whole episode was a rite of passage for Gregory, a risk forced on his honor by his peers – the next stage, a proof.

In the middle of his terror, Don remembered the teenage boys he'd worked with several years before at the Transitional Living Program, a residential facility across the bay in St. Petersburg. Some had been in gangs and had wanted to escape them. They might be this man's age now, if they were still alive. For a moment, Don wondered if Gregory had been among them. He wondered if, perhaps, Gregory knew him somehow. Perhaps he was student at the university?

To give Gregory the money in his wallet, Don picked up his jeans from the floor.

"Slow," Gregory said.

That voice, almost a chalky substance – Don believes still that he could identify it with greater confidence than the man's face.

The wallet, Don remembered, was on his desk in the study down the hall. He tried to look up at Gregory, thinking – the improbable optimist – that he might need to identify him. But Don saw only the man's waist – almost a camera angle out of Spielberg's *E.T.*, the child's view of the adult world. Don saw Gregory's light brown leather gloves, standard hardware store issue.

Then the man stepped back (he must have stepped back, though neither Lisa nor Don remembers), and they were to pass in front of him down the hallway to the money.

• • • • • • • • • • •

Suddenness is all the minutes turning their hydra heads toward you at once.

It is a constancy for which no person has a like capacity.

It surrounds and confounds. It is a ceaseless tipping point, always on the move, invisible until it falls to you.

Don finds himself drawn to consider the state of suddenness because it seems an almost parallel dimension to the ordinary in any individual life.

With this in mind, he thinks first, these days, of the attacks on the World Trade Center and Washington, or, more precisely, the thirst of one young man on that dire morning – though, of course, he could choose any other instant or character to consider. Like many, Don did not understand, at first, the seriousness of the attacks. But before he knew it (the expression itself acknowledges the slippage that accompanies suddenness) he found himself at the university, where all classes had been canceled and a makeshift counseling center had been set up in a Gilded Age ballroom that one of the national cable news companies routinely turns into a studio to present Florida focus groups. On the television monitors there, a network anchor intoned with his sleeves rolled to connote the shared seriousness of the situation – and its suddenness. Several of Don's colleagues, some of them administrators and psychologists, looked on, grimly. Only a handful of students were present and among these was a young man weeping. His father worked in one of the WTC towers now billowing smoke. He had been unable to contact family in New York to discover his father's whereabouts.

One of the psychologists had tried to encourage and console the young man and then had retreated. A short while later, he asked Don to try to make further contact. The young man sat with an equally young, pierced woman who stared ahead, having said all she could say, apparently. Don sat down beside them and thought of his colleague in the career center upstairs urging him that morning to "be gentle" with his classes, since most of the students, she said, were really no more than kids. He thought of his mordant reply, "So should I tell them the righteous have been wronged and leave it at that?"

The young man wept unselfconsciously, and Don tried, without success, to speak. As this silence seemed to knot itself, Don grew alarmed at his place in its coils, recalling a night in China years before when he had stood, wordless and unable to act, at the bedside of a fellow expatriate writhing in a devastating fever, until a mutual friend told him softly, firmly, "You're not helping. Why don't you just go."

"Can I get you something?" Don said to the young man, at last.

"Yeah," the young man sighed, sniffling. "Maybe a Pepsi."

Don hustled down the hall to the soda machine. Empty. He raced across the parking lot to the next nearest machine. Empty. So here he was in the glare of suddenness, nearly frantic, determined, dashing toward the student union two blocks away, sweating in the September heat, his mind like millions of others maddening slowly on the prospect of distant smoke. Here he was, threading the calm foot traffic, the traffic of dorm-room flirtation and letter grades, as though his eternal unforeseeable role in the universe was this feverish searching out. Then he found a stocked soda dispenser and returned to the ballroom with the people seated before televised buildings now collapsing, and he handed the can of sugared water to a boy weeping so long into a white paper napkin it had crumbled onto the useless cell phone in his lap.

. . . .

> "Otherness" is not a choice. It's recognized by
> the affliction it brings to the encounter.
> Composure is the habit of a caged silence.
> You are not mine. We are not a pair.

. . . .

When Don thinks of suddenness, he thinks also of his brother-in-law, a hospital nurse, who once cared for a terribly ill diabetic – a demanding, bitter, frightened middle-aged man, keen to assert and insult. After many days of abuse, Don's brother-in-law – usually a reserved man – finally told the patient off and kept his distance during the remainder of his shift.

He arrived at the ward the next morning to find that the man had died in the night. The body had already been taken for an autopsy. The attending pathologist invited him to the morgue to view it and, as they were discussing the corpse's condition, put its heart in his hands.

So what dimension is it where you hold the weight that yesterday cursed you, that you cursed?

. . . .

For years, Don has tried, with varying degrees of success, to understand how rage consorts with suddenness – in order to prevent its woeful damages. In 1996, for instance, frustrated with his more rational attempts at self-control and self-improvement, he wrote a letter to himself by pretending to write to that passion. Some passages:

> *Where are you now, who have ranted at a thou-*
> *sand suns that you shine brighter? Who have*

marched off madly with monumental wounds
into moonless night, ignorant of the way back?
Who have plunged your puzzled heart into
whiskey and prose? You, who have pressed your
sweet knife to the throat of love, commanding:
Say as I do.

You have leaned into my mirror with such
utter conviction, such shame, such boredom.
You, seducer of reason, progenitor of good res-
olutions. You, blind horse in a burning barn.

Is this how you seem to the eyes you con-
front, the wills you must defeat? I have loved
you like a son his battering father. I have
received you like the high in the needle. And
habit has taught me to need you.

Mercurial, you can vanish as quickly as you
appear. You pass through walls and best intentions. You inveigle by storm. You snatch the
moment up in your jaws to break its neck.

My shape-shifter, you never change.

I hear your footsteps. The air around me
prickles with some imminent charge. And I
fail to believe it's you bolting forth. You are ex-
pert at escalation. Patient, like a fallen pine
snagging and unsnagging its way downstream.
Alert, like an agent closing the land deal from
the first greeting. Yet you devour your own
entrails, in every incarnation. The smell is inescapable.

You have no memory but what serves your
thrust. The future is to you a valley grateful for

your pillaging. The present is always simple. . . .

*. . . I shouldn't be so proprietary about you.
Except that would let you roam blamelessly,
some essence on the trade winds of breath, a
chemical gush, what you do next and what
you've done. . . .*

*. . . I have seen water dumped on grease fire,
and souls swimming in that matter, some trying to smile. You are with them now, too. And
with those others whose whirlings and roars
squeeze the laughter of smugness from me,
those who never learn, just as I haven't. And
with those others, somehow related to me, who
open the ledger of species evil and begin their
entry. . . .*

*. . . You cannot flatter me now, cannot give
me the right. I want you to be more memorable than a smoldering battlement. I want you
to paint your difficulty. Be the cobra I entrance
with three slow kisses on the nose.*

*This is no appeal, my naive spook. The curse
is on.*

As excessive as this invocation might sound in its poetic agitation, it points to a longing for composure. A curse is a vain
beggar's stratagem, and by conferring names on certain kinds of
unmanageable surprise here, Don is hoping to forestall them
forever and relieve himself of his own terrifying suddenness
and shame. Desperately he wishes to turn an old shouting into
eloquence, or at least to kill it by making it acceptably cunning.
Perhaps that is why he writes part of this book in third person

31

and why he remains curious about Gregory's composure in the bedroom. How surprised could Gregory have been by what he encountered there?

• • • • • • • • • • •

I want you dead, every bit of you. And it seems I want that killing for myself. Get it? I think about it over shepherd's pie at lunch, on the porch beside the orange blossoms, walking from my poetry class. My breath catches as I see you enter the bedroom, beside the head-board of the bed. I stand at the opposite corner of the bed, and the gun is in my hand, heavy, bright. A forty-five. I, who own no gun, who've only hunted a little with shotguns in boyhood … suddenly I know how to hold it. I fire, three times, I let you have it. I hit you in the head. Blood pops out like a rash thought and you fall, you fall back through a Hollywood movie villain death.

But there is no release.

Because you fire back at me. I'm hit. I'm not hit. It's never clear. I fire again and again, and you drop dead. The blood spatters the walls. You're there, on the floor and I'm scared to approach but I do, and I kick you in the ribs. I kick you a second time. . . .

And sometimes Lisa is shot. . . .

But most often I fire and you stop, surprised yet unfazed. You're wearing a flack jacket – of course, why didn't I realize that? –

and you are simply not affected. Or I fire and
miss you, again and again. You fall, and when I
approach, you grab my ankle from your red
mess. I was a fool to have trusted in your
death. . . .

Or you stand over me at the foot of the bed
and bring out a knife, and we are wrestling,
my pink cock wagging. You and your clothes.
Who will knee the other first? Will it matter?
Who is stronger? Who will fall on whom?

And then wrapped in a bed sheet, I stagger,
bleeding, into the front yard I've complained
about and worked in, my land of the broken
sprinkler pipe and the shaggy plumbago, that
place from which I've watched so many people
pass on foot to and from the grocery store at
the end of the street.

• • • • • • • • • • •

Thirteen days after the Zantops were murdered, a forensic pathologist paraphrased by a *Valley News* reporter conjectured that
whoever killed them "most likely exploded into a fit of rage
when he stabbed them . . . and probably left behind a scene he
hoped would make a statement." The pathologist went on to hy-
pothesize that because the murders were committed during the
day, the killer did not plan the attack but "acted on angry impulse." The choice of a knife as murder weapon suggested the
"deepest kind of anger."

. . . .

Maybe our nakedness made it obvious that we were helpless? Maybe it made abducting one or both of us a hassle? Maybe our submissiveness was the perfect turnoff?

We've never been untouched this way.

. . . .

When Lisa and Don contemplate the timing of Gregory's arrival, they shudder through the ugly outcomes of each having been home alone with him. But that unease swirls away in the stir of wondering, again, about whether they had been watched, perhaps even studied, by their intruder.

On Saturday, after I had returned from some errands, I discovered Lisa waiting for me in the driveway, wearing a new dress – a consignment store special. It was an unusual dress for her – big with roses – and over it she wore a linen jacket, which she allowed to fall tantalizingly (parodically) from one shoulder. She swiveled and mocked the model who might stare past the camera with divine vacancy. And the dusty driveway seemed as incongruous as one of the absurd backdrops for fashion photos in the *Times* – those that appall by their unapologetic indifference to the pieties screaming from the irony of tall ingénues in $1,500 boots towering over astonished and worshipful indigents at a soup kitchen beneath an expressway bridge.

I was surprised by the dress, pleased that she would wear it to dinner that evening – proud of her in it, proud of her romantic inspiration and excitement to parade. She looked good there.

And, on the back side of this happy moment, I wondered who might be watching us then? And how long had they been watching, and to what end? When people fantasize about being looked at, they most often assume, groundlessly, that they control the eyes of the onlooker and the meanings derived from this peculiar captivity.

How could you know I didn't have a gun?

How could you dare come down our hallway not knowing?

In those first days after you appeared, my terrored mind sometimes imagined you were our neighbor from across the street. Didn't he drive up shortly after it happened? Isn't the upstairs room of his house high enough that, with binoculars, he could have spied us on our bed? Hadn't the blind been up on our porch window?

Lisa said this morning that she awoke last night with the melody to "Love and Marriage" running through her head but with a substitute lyric: "Rape and murder, rape and murder. . . ."

I glance at the back door almost every time I pass through the hallway. At night, I nearly expect your shadow to appear on the other side of the shade. I loathe the shades drawn, the windows locked – enclosed, enclosing. We peer out from behind the blinds before we draw them open. We do this casually, quickly, as though we are not that timid.

On the radio now a program about "snitch culture" reports that there are recurring protests in Berlin about the use of web cam surveillance in public places. The circle of privacy, the spokesman declares, has drawn tighter around us. I recall how I seemed to be the only one at our health club who was the least troubled when management decided to install monitoring equipment that required us to punch in a numeric code and present our right hands to a computer eye in order to lift weights.

Our house is wired with electronic alarms, and the sign stating such stands in the front yard. The alarms were turned off on your Sunday afternoon. There is a neighborhood watch group. Where were their eyes that day? It's true. Lisa and I have never attended their meetings.

Later, during that same radio program (on the commercial-free community station), a woman argues against consumerism, against substituting the acquisition of more goods for "expressiveness and connection." She claims that we deny our fear through consumerism and that we need to "befriend" our fear, and come thereby to understand our real feelings.

How could you not have been carrying a weapon?

. . . .

During a dinner debate between two of Lisa and Don's friends, it is asserted that anecdotal evidence, though sometimes vivid, is nothing but a sentimental appeal compared to the larger and truer pattern of reality provided by statistics. Don recalls to himself the dubious data on home invasions and a recent report – again from the local community radio station – about a U.S. tobacco company trying to convince several Eastern European countries to open their markets to its brand of cigarettes. The tobacco company had argued that the increased numbers who will die early from smoking-related illness will actually reduce overall health care costs to the state, because such costs are higher for citizens who survive to an average life expectancy.

What shall it be? Numbers over story? Correlation over dialogue?

And, yet, how they entwine!

For instance, when we hope for safety – when we flee, say, from the likelihood that the found tumor is malignant – don't we seek to place ourselves amid the large, untroubled number we envision lumbering untouched through the days? And isn't this just the reverse of our hopes when we purchase the lottery ticket, or when we dream of stardom and actually pursue it?

Don considers the code for his house alarm. A bland, self-indulgent number, perhaps, since it didn't help. He thinks of the words, "the death toll may reach three thousand," and of the disparate claims of every account. He thinks of Lisa confiding to her friend about Gregory several weeks after the invasion, "I can't get it into my head that it happened, and I can't get it out of my head." He sees the obituaries in the *Times* of those killed at the World Trade Center attack, the poignant insistence in the redundant, lonely phrases, in the blurred and incongruously cheerful photos, that individual identity matters, at least in death, in this kind of death, as though any two deaths were the same.

Face and the want of a face. Just after the attack, there was the story of a man in the WTC – a man most assuredly invented – who had told somebody who had told somebody that he'd met the eye of one of the hijacker-pilots an instant before the airliner swept upward and slammed into the floor above his.

And, of course, the killers themselves were eager to matter, avid for that paradise. Their poor photos, too, haunted the *Times* (those of whom there were photos), pitched beside the photos of those deemed their monstrous mentors – faces, it was declared, of evil.

Don hears Lisa say into the phone, "Every morning when I go to my closet, I pass through a crime scene." Is personal experience not grotesque, a special sort of number? On the day after the invasion, when he returned to the house, Don cleaned up as much shattered glass as he could. He collected and boxed the scattered pieces of the back door – an interior door, he soon discovered – and washed his hands, and sat down at the piano to invest the atmosphere with some familiar body. A few minutes later, however, he thought he heard a strange sound and crept to the back of the house to investigate. It was the neighbor dog dragging a metal bowl. Returning to the piano, Don jumped in fright at the sight of a black towel on the piano bench. How could he have forgotten he'd tossed it there a few minutes before, what his panic had transformed for a moment into a wadded shadow?

38

Neither Don nor Lisa were wearing their eyeglasses when Gregory came. (In fact, there is some disagreement between them about Gregory not wearing a mask. Lisa sometimes suggests, with varying conviction, that a nylon stocking obscured his features.) Don wonders over and over at Gregory's face, which he cannot make out, because he cannot raise his gaze in memory above the level of Gregory's belt. Yet an eye persists in Don's mind, a wide, white-ringed, sidelong glaring eye of a cartoon gangster-wolf from his childhood. He doesn't ask himself what it might see.

Instead, he reminds himself to lift his tongue from the pit of his mouth and then slip it between his teeth so they cannot be clenched and further infuriate the nerves of his jaw clicking and creaking and screwing a fine pin of pain into his ear, his countenance contorting then without his knowledge, as though something in the air were deforming it while the recollected encounter with his own killing is again underway.

. . . .

From the bedroom, Gregory had Lisa and Don lead him down the hallway to Don's study. Don still sees himself, as they move, hunching like a small child just out of the swimming pool on a chilly morning, the knobs of his backbone protruding. How close was Gregory to the bare back? Don did not think of it, could not think of it, though the image barges into his mind now over and over. The bareness – where the knife could have gone.

They stood around the desk in Don's study. Don slipped the money from his wallet, his hands wagging as though devastated by Parkinson's disease. Gregory picked up Don's keys from among the papers and paraphernalia of dailiness. Even so close – how close? – Don did not look up at him.

39

Again, Gregory had them move past him, back down the hall toward the bedroom. Lisa was between the men. Horrified by the proximity to Gregory, she scurried ahead of Don, clutching Don's wadded shirt to her chest.

"Don't run," he commanded.

He marched them into the bathroom – Lisa's bathroom, actually, since Don had ceded it to her when they first moved in after finding the sight of his bald spot in the mirrors inescapable while seated on the toilet there. It was a room he rarely entered, one of her places, laden with brushes and cosmetics, and decorated more or less by the previous owners, he liked to tell visitors, in a style somewhere between a 19th-century boarding house and the old-time Hollywood idea of a harem.

Gregory commanded them to crouch in front of the tub – their picturesque antique tub, original to the house. He closed the door behind him. With the window heavily shaded and the lights off, the room was dim. Could they all hear the next-door neighbor children playing in their front yard, thirty feet away, shrieking, laughing? Don and Lisa looked up at him, straining to see. Gregory cupped one hand over the other, like a bodyguard beside a podium, or a minister about to make an announcement. He seemed as dark as the mouth of a cave.

"Now I have to tie you up," he said.

. . . .

Don was raised in a "quiet neighborhood" – that is, from his reading and from television, he came to believe that he lived a dull life and, as such, it did not test him as a person who encountered the ultimate knowledge of his epoch should be tested. In his apprehension of this belief – one more in a long train of contemporary provincial commonplaces – he was as a child of most epochs. And, after he had grown up, had he continued to wish for the remote, specialized sufferings to which he had been superficially introduced, had he longed for such as adventures, he would have been only a fool. Instead he became a traveler, and by this an advanced somnambulist, his eyes wide open in the dreaming of spectatorship and imagination.

He carried what one of his friends in Poland once called his "golden American passport" with a secret, divided pride – with the measured assurance of one who knows it will open all but a few foreign gates, some of which will be eagerly welcoming and others bitter, even dangerous, in their accommodation, and with justification. Nearly everywhere he went, he discovered a little of the America that had made its way there before him – arriving via film or CD, in weaponry or fashion or sports stardom, in the remembered figures of liberators or occupiers, employers or exploiters, silent operatives of various sorts, even as teachers – and he hoped not to be implicated personally by whatever wrongs nested in those histories. He wished to be taken as an individual, not as a representative or symbol. Nonetheless, he was also flattered to be mistaken for a Canadian or European – and, thus, somehow not reviled for stereotypical American ignorance and arrogance abroad, nor envied for assumed personal wealth, however slight it might actually be, and the blindness conferred by privilege.

At home, however, Don had been too little aware of the suddenness around him – not even understanding, for instance, why his first lover kept a pistol under her pillow.

The quiet neighborhood is always the puzzle in the eyes of witnesses to supreme suddenness. The Zantops' friends and neighbors, fellow citizens of tidy, well-endowed villages far, for the present, from catastrophic history (the kinds of villages

41

where the doors, they insisted in their fidelity to mythic peace, had remained unlocked at night) – these people could not believe what had befallen their community. And they were not alone in this, for it is a standard, this disbelief, perhaps even an ancient adaptive principle. One could argue that illusion, walled horizons, half-truths and, in some instances, lies deepen communal wounds with a particular strain of infectious anger, a keen drive for resolution at any cost. Certainly, they can fortify what is most suspiciously untouchable in grief and fear, and inhibit the chance of healing.

More difficult for the community than accepting that the murders had changed things, perhaps forever – and that satisfactory answers or redeeming insight might never be forthcoming – was the eventual revelation that the killers were from among them: a pair of clumsy teenagers, Robert Tulloch and James Parker. The evidence against them was so overwhelming that it seemed they wanted to be caught, though they had fled town after the killings and, later, claimed they had committed the crime as part of their plan to acquire ATM cards and, thus, enough money to go to Australia.

The Zantops were travelers, too – and of course they were international. According to their friends, they were hard-working idealists. They wanted to make the world a better place, beginning with home. They opened their door to that prospect. They trusted.

•　•　•　•　•　•　•　•　•　•

Sometimes, when I let myself think it, I almost
believe I invited your invasion by not replacing
that tiny padlock on the back gate with one
heavier and more suitable for the job. That small

padlock had been latched on my backpack for years, in all my travels over Asia and Africa, and elsewhere, and it had discouraged thieves, apparently.

Someone had tried pulling the back gate open once or twice in the past year but hadn't succeeded, so I left that lock on there. I haven't told Lisa about this.

I am trying to fill in your absence, which is like a promise.

Your presence is a blankness outlined by the fine line of vivid detail, the remains of your appearance. If this figure were in, say, a coloring book, I could wonder whether I were keeping my speculations within the lines. How could I determine my trespasses, if that's what they would be? They're all trespasses, in or outside the lines.

I imagine you throwing yourself through the doors of other houses. Sometimes those doors are unlocked and you merely walk in. And you've arrived to finish the business. Sometimes you are waiting for me to enter the room and turn on the lamp, seated on the couch, say, or smoking in a chair.

Were you experienced? Whom did you tell about us, if you did? If you could?

You come to me like the dead. You, beggar. You, homeless in a way you couldn't have meant.

The vision of encountering you again is as stubborn and resourceful as the first heartbreak.

• • • • • • • • • • •

"You know he had to have a gun," one of Don's friends insists. "A gun makes people brave, not a knife."

If so, Gregory had been judicious about showing it. Florida is a ten-twenty-life state. As a billboard near an expressway in Tampa succinctly declares: Carry a gun while committing a crime, and it's ten years in prison. Fire it, and it's twenty. Hurt or kill someone, and it's life.

"Damn, bro," said the carpenter who replaced the dolly with a new, exterior door, refitted with unpullable pins, refitted also to swing outward. He had been the twentieth person to hear the story of the crime in forty-eight hours. By then, Don had learned how to shorten and focus the tale.

"Too bad you didn't have a gun to blast that sucker," the carpenter said, shaking his head. "What are you gonna do?"

Changing the keys and dead bolts that same day, the locksmith told Don that he was robbed at gunpoint several years before, as he was coming out of a convenience store. The gunman made the locksmith drive him around for three hours. Then he told the locksmith to get out of the car – he was stealing it.

"No," the locksmith told the gunman, "get out or shoot me now."

(As he related this incident to Don, he added, "I was having a major anxiety attack.")

"You must be crazy," the gunman said.

"No," the locksmith replied, "I've just had it. You got $400 from me, go. Go."

The gunman got out and walked away.

"I thought about running him down," the locksmith told Don, his countenance sleepy, as though snowflakes weighted his eyelashes, "but they'd probably get me for vehicular homicide."

. . . .

On those airliners, after the hijackers with
their box cutters have taken over the cabin, an
unsuspected passenger pulls a pistol from his
briefcase (a smuggled pistol for just such an
emergency), and he blasts the three intimida-
tors into oblivion, without rupturing the
cabin. He busts down the cockpit door and
pulls back the seats and shoots their partners,
shoots them good. . . .

How many like me, all over the country,
suddenly stock-still in the shower before another day on the job, how many try to dream
that gun into that briefcase there? How many
want to pull it out (I can almost feel it now)
and use it themselves?

And when will this futility end?

It occurs to me now you couldn't have
handled a pistol while wearing those work
gloves. You must have had a knife.

At dinner with some people we've just met,
one rigorously tailored woman told us about
confronting a man climbing through her window.

"I thought about killing him," she said,
"but instead I shot him in the knee." Then she
added, to make it clear to us, "I showed mercy."

I smoke a cigar on the back deck. There's
the door I've painted white, the replacement
door, its bottom half reinforced wood but the

top half lattice windows, since we will not
give up all our afternoon light to you.

What kind of man paints such a door? Does
Lisa feel I am competent to paint such a door?
I know I cannot protect her from a thing. I
never assumed I was a protector. I am a verified nonprotector. I am a verified quiverer.
And this is an illusion, the power to take and
relinquish power as I will.

Declarations of my submissiveness to you
must embarrass some men. (I suppose it
strengthens me to admit it in their presence.)
One acquaintance stops me on campus, and I
tell him the story, interrupted by a bombastic
turboprop circling overhead, trailing an ad–
vertisement. As I speak, he grits his teeth and
seems nearly ready to weep. I wonder, stupidly, if some of his Viet Nam experience is
surfacing as post-traumatic stress. His wince
is true – so much so he wants to get away from
it – and it's sweet, his real gift, sealed with a
double handshake, as though he were helping
me to steady an unruly rudder.

Last night at the dance concert at the university, one of my office enemies approached
me with some consolation. He'd just heard
of the invasion. He was serious and plain. I
thanked him. He told a story of his childhood
dog crashing though the glass of the back door
and clamping on the thigh of an intruder preparing to break in. We quickly fell to jokes.

I mentioned that I had been naked when you arrived, so you could be assured I had no weapon.

"You had one," my office foe laughed, seeming now a paltry foe.

"Yeah," I replied, sharing the levity, "but it wasn't the kind that could do me any good."

. . . .

Lisa fantasizes of the escapes she and Don did not attempt.

Why didn't they run screaming through their bedroom doors onto the porch when they first heard Gregory crashing into the house? Why didn't they slam their bedroom door shut and shove the bed in front of it?

She also wonders why, when crouching before Gregory in the bedroom, she didn't grab the hammer from the Chinese box there behind her? Or low in the dim bathroom, she could have snatched up the spray can of Lysol from beside the toilet, and blasted it into Gregory's eyes.

Six months later, nine months later, she still notices the objects in her house that could alter fates should they be used as weapons.

It bothers her when Don leaves for work before she does. When he goes away overnight on business, she goes away, as well, to her mother's or to visit friends. She admits to disliking 4 p.m.

"He had no right to an experience like that," she says of Gregory.

She recalls how she and Don slept in their clothes for days after they first came back into the house.

"Look at us," she'd said, in disgust.

They'd inspected all the closets before they'd turned in for the night.

"I know this is crazy," she'd said after he'd shut off the light and climbed in beside her, "but I've got to check under the bed."

Don slid from between the covers and searched below.

"Well?" she'd asked.

"Just a mad goat dozing."

Friends had given them sage to burn – as the Native Americans once did, they said – in the four corners of the house, to banish evil spirits and reclaim their place. The odor of that smoke – magical thinking, Don mused, from some sentimental notion of a wiser tribe than theirs, a tribe long ago exterminated.

He and Lisa followed that smoke from room to room and were grateful for it. They had considered selling the house but then had gotten angrier and stubborn. Instead, they had entertained more often.

They'd noticed that society seemed to have given them three months to speak of Gregory, and then no more. Such was the form assigned for public speech to accomplish its obscure task, and they were embarrassed to breach it, especially without a joke.

"Don't dismiss what happened to you," a psychologist-relative urged Don during a conversation at a family reunion. He had tried to diminish the invasion by comparing it to grander disasters and misfortunes. She told of one her patients who had been raped repeatedly by a captor. The woman was so cold and wrecked afterward, her assailant wrapped her in a big coat to comfort her. This gesture made her recovery more difficult because she was so grateful to him for not killing her and for this other "kindness."

One day, Lisa mentions to Don that she feels despondent, that now she can understand suicide, and this frightens her.

"He seemed to be letting it go slowly," she says of Gregory on another day, "deciding what to do with us."

On another day, she finds a sliver of glass from the back door, in the bottom of her briefcase.

. . . .

Don reads about studies on the chemistry of trauma, on what has been discovered about the jets of epinephrine that sluice through the brain during terror. The research asserts that much is unknown. One thing is certain: too much fear for too long, and the organism begins to tear itself down – as if it were fleeing bit by bit.

> We always hope that by understanding how
> things work we can control them. What's
> older in life than flight and pursuit? I guess I
> wanted to know what my feeling in those
> minutes with you – that feeling – was literally
> made of. As if a rainbow on a bubble were sim-
> ply light shot through water drops into a cer-
> tain kind of eye. There's something useful, yes,
> in understanding that much. But it's also
> strangely useless to think that you and Lisa
> and I are all just the same adrenaline, that
> we're identical at a given point. It makes me
> want to ask what the chemistry of poetic
> beauty is, or God hunger, or the chemistry, for
> instance, that inspires some people to secretly
> wish for vicarious disaster simply to break

49

their boredom. It makes me want to ask what the ultimate material processes are, the universal statistical mechanics that allow a person to say, with the most compassionate sincerity, to one in pain, "Why don't you go buy yourself something nice. This situation is at least worth a new sport coat, don't you think?"

· · · · · · · · · ·

Several months after Robert Tulloch and James Parker were apprehended and awaiting trial, a Northeastern University criminologist observed in the *Valley News*: "This was a crime that was senseless, and that's why so many people have trouble understanding it. . . . The evil part of this I believe is the relationship between these two boys. I don't think either of them would have done this by himself. It was the chemistry between them and the bond they shared."

A criminologist from Reading, Vermont, offered: "The only way we will truly know is if they tell us."

· · · · · · · · · ·

On September 22, 2001, seven months after Gregory and eleven days after the attacks on the WTC and the Pentagon, Lisa received a letter postmarked September 18 from Denver, Colorado. The envelope contained a triangular piece of paper that unfolded into a slightly larger triangle, a sliced corner of common bond. On it was typed:

> Travel nurses make us ill
> They really are a drag.
> Instead of treating and healing us,
> All they do is bitch and nag.

They make more dollars
Than they should,
Though to hear it they're downtrodden.
Hate is etched into their greedy hearts,
Are they chummy with bin Laden.

Cheers

The address on the envelope was typed, as well.

Months later, Lisa still wonders what "travel nurse" means. She remembers that some weeks before this mailing arrived she received a phone call asking if she was a registered nurse. She guesses that another Lisa Birnbaum who is a nurse might have a dissatisfied client.

"Or maybe it's intended for me because Birnbaum is a Jewish name?"

She and Don let this apparent hate letter mean as little as they dare, putting it aside until a few weeks later when letters laced with anthrax began to appear around the country, most notably in the offices of a network news anchor and the Senate majority leader. Both of these letters, it was revealed, were also post-marked on September 18. But they contained a white powder, in which the anthrax spores had been nested, and Lisa's letter did not.

Lisa admits to feeling "numb" in general. I
told her I felt as though we were separated and
yet allies, on parallel tracks.

Her nightmare last night: "We were in a
house open to the whole world, to everything.
And we were in the shower and heard him
coming. And you jumped out of the shower
and crouched behind the door, though that

51

wasn't going to stop him. Then you got back into the shower, and we were there. Then a hand came in toward us."

That was the point at which she had shouted and woke. This morning she said, "I see you must be crouching with this thing, too."

I replied, "I'm writing this, these pages, to help myself stand up."

The U.S. bombing of Afghanistan continues. Food packets, we are told, are also being dropped, for citizens there. A headline from a column of the local paper here: "People Will Decide War's Name Despite Official Label."

The insecurity of America – now with the fear of anthrax or other lethal agents: I can't help feeling that it's another form of you, multiplied, expanded.

And yet, if you are still here in Tampa, aren't you afraid that we might already be exposed to anthrax, or worse? Is it coming soon, the terrible thing that is always promised to come soon? After all, we live just a few miles from Central Command, MacDill Air Force Base – from which America's recent wars have been directed. Doesn't that make us casualties-in-waiting beside *the* military target? Doesn't our very ordinariness mark us?

. . . .

Several days after Lisa received the hate letter, an employee of the Florida tabloid the *Sun* died of anthrax sent in the mail, as did several postal workers in Washington DC and a ninety-four-year-old woman in Massachusetts – though no one could discover how the woman became infected since all in her local post office tested negative for the spores. These incidents were, of course, spores of a different order, and the fear they carried sometimes found expression in improbable corners. Employees at a post office in India, for instance, began itching after a suspicious piece of mail had been cited, but the envelope in question contained only a greeting card.

Lisa and Don thought they might report the letter to the police, but the police had seemed indifferent about Gregory once the main investigator on the case learned that Gregory had been wearing gloves. How then, Lisa and Don reasoned, could the police help them with this letter if they couldn't begin to find Gregory?

"It's too bad they won't let us electrify our fences," the main police investigator had said with a sigh, almost to himself, as he looked around Don and Lisa's back deck, his hands in his pockets. "That would slow the guy down. . . . But I wouldn't worry. He's gone back to whatever hole he crawled out of."

Lisa and Don had refrained from touching anything in the house before the police arrived, hoping this would aid the investigation. It seemed that all five or six officers walked around with their hands in their pockets except for one, a left-hander, who was filling out the crime incident form.

On the other side of you lies habit, chores, and the obligations to my former life until the moment when that life was called into question. On the other side of the terror: story, summation, forgetting, clinging unwholesomely to certain details. The terror . . . then the viscous drip of bureaucracy . . . the forms and phone numbers and file numbers and policy numbers. Numbers! How many degrees of horror are coursing though each moment in America? How many blades across how many yards of human flesh? How many ghostly dialogues begun?

The insurance agent requests the incident report. I call the police for a copy. The woman tells me it's ready, I can pick it up. (I'm surprised it isn't being sent, or that the officer did not give me a copy on site.)

The police department records office – have you been there? – is decorated for Valentine's Day with pink hearts and bears and rabbits carrying signs that declare, "I love you." Along the wall a more permanent mosaic depicts the history of Tampa. Its theme is progress, from the taking of the land from the natives to the age of rocketry. (The story stops at 1960, when the office was built, presumably.) Small ironies everywhere – they are the ironies engendered by the accoutrements and pro forma gestures of

goodness and civility and the boosterism of
clean towns.

My incident report costs me forty-five cents.
In line ahead of me, a woman hands money to
her small boy so that he may pass it to the clerk.

"He likes to pay," she explains to me.

The clerk gives me only the first page of my
report, "since the case is under investigation."
A detective will call. I notice that Lisa's age has
been incorrectly entered on the form – a year in
the favor of youth. The courtesy of the officer's
unconscious?

• • • • • • • • • • •

The large event reawakens the voice of the
smaller event, and we discover that the smaller
event is not small at all. There is no such thing
as smallness when listening to the voice of life,
the voice of a single mortality.

It's that bubble that fills and fills. A person
thinks he knows it and all it contains. He
thinks it's too much for him. He thinks he
wants to lie down and sleep because it's so frag-
ile and bearing so much. But this is merely his
introduction to the sleepy starvation of the
world, the shouting in the dust for change and
the hope for that change, and the idiotic fun
and despairing anger of shooting up the village
in the meantime . . . the headache in the morning after . . . the emptied tongue of the grieving
mother. . . .

• • • • • • • • • •

Tasteless and odorless, the anthrax spores.

The night bombing in Afghanistan continues. Ordinary people are dying, at the far edges of news stories. Of course they are.

Many Afghan troops surrender, many sides changing.

Osama bin Laden is said to be sleeping in caves, fleeing, hunted. Anytime he will be captured or killed. Anytime. Soon. Soon.

". . . back to whatever hole he crawled out of. . . ."

One report mentions an uprising among foreign prisoners of war after they have given themselves up. There is the suggestion that they might have been encouraged to rebel, so that they could be killed.

On another day – what day is it? – there is a massacre of Christians in a church in Pakistan. The assassins ride up on motorcycles and shoot sixteen or seventeen dead, including the pastor. The journalist at the scene says that some of the killed had begged for their lives.

Don thinks of the girder pulled from the wreckage of the WTC three weeks after the attack – still red-hot.

On the public radio station, he hears the propaganda voices of "Islamic extremists" shouting *Down with America! Down with America!* The voices, he assumes, of poor, mostly ignorant and easily-incited young men. Now he gazes across the parking lot of the supermarket in the "upscale" neighborhood adjacent to his district – a supermarket that has more solicitous service and a better selection of fresh fish than the store at the end of his street. He hears those voices and regards the well-dressed men and women who have stopped in, like him, for a few things on the way home from a day at their offices.

He's heard those angry voices before. Who hasn't? He knows better. And yet the temptation to want them dead at any price – yes! – to keep them far from this parking lot. To do anything to silence them – who are they, really? – and to keep this evening, the dinner to come, the peace, such as it is. He steps from his car, and as he enters the supermarket he now hears the recorded rock and roll music blaring from the soup kitchen for indigents set up beneath the freeway bridge across the river.

• • • • • • • • • •

A week later, a young woman sits down next to Don amid the wailing and sneezing of a doctor's waiting room. (Don is there for a routine physical.) A moment later, she leaves her purse on the couch between him and an older man while she goes out to her car, Don presumes, for some article. As the minutes elapse and she does not return, however, trepidation wriggles through Don, in spite of himself. Why, he wonders, would a woman leave a bomb on a couch in a medical office in south Tampa, as though this were, for instance, Jerusalem? One could as well ask why someone would send a hate letter, or a package with a little suggestive powder sprinkled on it. Perhaps such speculations will not seem solipsistic and sentimental a few years hence, should we enter the age of op-ed by nuclear device.

Don glances down at the tiny, embroidered clutch. His left ear seems to ring, and he tries to resist the sensation. He envisions metal tearing into his rib cage. Should we suggest that some long-held but ungrasped knowledge of the world at large has, at last, taken hold of him?

He rises and strolls eight feet to the water cooler, turning away from the suddenness about to occur.

As he drinks, the young woman strides back into the room with the item she has gone out to fetch – a nursing textbook.

. . . .

Some people ask, "Did the experience change your ideas about God? Did it make you religious?"

Let's not sentimentalize the possibility of being changed by events. For a while, Lisa and I told ourselves that certain things "didn't matter anymore," things like money and how punctually certain deadlines are met – and this is true, to a point. We have enough manic adherence to squander – and perhaps we have been stingy with ourselves in the past. But while I might remain calmer than usual about frustrations, I don't believe that having encountered you voids much that we invested with worth (or stupid sorrow, or avoidable suffering). Encountering you only redefines everything in life from time to time, and maybe for a few minutes only.

What would it take to change you? What did it take to make you?

In the days immediately after you came, I was thankful and yet too shocked to actually verify that I felt thankful. My gratitude was intellectual, an act of good manners in the house of the cosmos.

Most thankfulness is an agitating relief. It is insufficiency personified in the face of all the doors smashed down by all the Huns of existence.

. . . .

"Now I have to tie you up."

> For some time after you came, the dark face
> on the street near my neighborhood, or that
> ghostly figure behind the tinted car glass
> throbbing with a hip-hop bass line, inspired
> the question: Are you the one? Are you him?
>
> This is not the question I should be asking,
> is it?
>
> In McDonald's, as I take money from the
> ATM, I glance repeatedly at a young man order-
> ing at the counter. He's short enough, perhaps
> stocky enough. I still have the look on my face
> when I get into my car, because a woman with
> her children stares at me intently as she gets
> out of hers. She actually pauses before she
> closes her car door, and I meet her stare, and
> there is nothing flirtatious in either of us. In-
> stead, it's bland intensity, a countenance that
> would seem a put-on were it not concentrated
> and unabashed, frank, somehow shutting out
> everything around us. When that contact
> breaks, I know I am weird. I have been judged
> so. I am one of those men, perhaps fearsome,
> of inscrutable but suspect preoccupation. I
> should be watched, at least a woman with kids
> thinks so. I glance at my face reflected in my
> driver's side window as I get in the car. It's a
> man's face – with a trace of the assurance, the
> alluring anger some men are reputed to pos-

sess, also a father's face, middle-aged, with furrows on the brow that appear to announce something important, as though they had been earned.

I think of our neighbor – I'll call him Fred – who pulled into his driveway a few minutes after the police had arrived silently from all directions at once and seemed to coast to a stop. Fred had an interest in our invasion, and in you. He sauntered across the street and asked what happened – our first verbal exchange in the years we've lived on the block. Immediately, he pulled out his cell phone and called his roommate in the house and asked if he'd seen anything. The roommate, Fred reported to Lisa and me and the extra police milling about, had noticed my car fly out of the driveway, but he took little note of it, thinking I might be angry or just in a hurry. Fred asked us if there was anything he could do to help. He lingered, and then I understood. Though Tampa is vying to host the 2012 Olympics and the sophistication that might accompany becoming a little Atlanta, though it was even recently named one of the best cities in the country to live in if you are gay and under thirty, this is America – and the South – and Fred is black. He sees a different neighborhood than I see. He wanted to make sure that we understood who he was and who we were.

I wonder if the neighborhood he sees is
anything like the one in your eye.

Now he waves every time I encounter him,
and I wave back and regret our solicitousness.

One of the trainers at Lisa and Don's health club – a black man
who appears to be in his early thirties but is often eager to brag
that he is almost forty and the proud father of four children –
shook his head anxiously at the Afghanistan war on the row of
televisions suspended above the stair-step machines. He drifted
away from the group of other watchers and declared to the air, as
if saying were proving, "Hey, those Arabs, they aren't going to
bother us. Black people don't have nothing here. We're not the
ones in charge."

. . . .

A couple of weeks ago, as Lisa and I sat sipping
wine in the living room and catching up on
the day at the office and beyond, we saw,
through our front window, a muscular young
man striding up our street. He wore a scarlet
nylon cap, tight against his skull like a pirate's
bandana. Lisa had seen him once before, and
she'd noted then how he averted his face as he
passed. This time, he also seemed to look
away.

She would like him to be you. She thinks
that if she could coax him to reply to a simple
"Hi!" she could verify that he's you. She remembers your voice, as do I, very well. She
jokes that she would like to call out "Gregory!"

to that man, hoping you would answer and be revealed. But, of course, that could never happen, could it?

I saw that man again yesterday, walking down the street, past our house, still wearing the red nylon bandana. It struck me that I might keep a disposable camera near at hand, so that if I encountered him again, I might try to capture some evidence. He's passed our front window three times when I've been home, always wearing the red cap, and since he has at times carried groceries, I assume that's always the object of his journey.

Of course, what would this photographic evidence be evidence of?

Am I sure I would like him to be you?

* * * * * * * * * *

"Now I have to tie you up."

Remember – because it is easy to forget, since Don and Lisa were not murdered, and since past events can seem obvious and inevitable merely because they are concluded, however much uncompleted – remember the dimness of the bathroom with its shade drawn in the gray afternoon. Picture Gregory standing in front of the closed door, one hand over the other as he makes his announcement. Hear the faint chime of the children playing in the front yard next door. Admit most of all the absolute ambiguity of this moment of suddenness, and the excruciating awareness of things impending. It is vital to gaining whatever contact humans are allowed with the minutes indifferent to all they contain, remote from us because they are not ours alone, or because they are others' alone forever.

Gregory had not killed Don and Lisa in their bedroom. He had not incapacitated Don as he followed the couple down the hallway to Don's wallet, which contained sixty dollars. Perhaps he had noticed Don's gathering of love notes from Lisa thumbtacked on the bulletin board of Don's study. Perhaps he had regarded the shelves of faintly mildewed books there and wondered about them. Perhaps he had assessed matters at hand and was trying to move Don and Lisa into a place where he could keep them quiet and more controlled for the true beginning of his invasion.

What had been decided? What had been intended? Where had it begun, and where would it conclude? What was tipping this way and that?

Consider the minutes just before the first of the 9/11 attackers signals his accomplices and reaches for the box cutter in his pocket.

Consider the minutes just before Robert Tulloch and James Parker pull out their knives.

Don and Lisa – anyone, aware or not – crouching before what was about to be done.

• • • • • • • • • •

At dinner, one of Don and Lisa's oldest friends, a man in his late fifties, a New York liberal, who has contemplated retiring to Costa Rica, rebukes Don for his spontaneous, patriotic rage at the WTC murderers:

"Don't tell me you think our government actually cares about us. They probably let 9/11 happen. One way or the other, the boardroom fascists in Washington haven't missed a beat since it all came down. We, the middle class, we're the ones who must be silenced now to make the new world order, whatever that is, run

63

as it must. We're the ones the national security creeps have to get into shape because we're the only ones with any real leverage to stand against them for human rights and due process and equal protection under the law. We have to be made to forget how things have been here in the States, the Bill of Rights and all that. I'm afraid America as it was, if it ever was, is as obsolete as Islam for the world that's coming. I'm also afraid enough now to think obsolescence of that sort is preferable to what the world at large has in store for us."

●　●　●　●　●　●　●　●　●　●　●

Afternoon. I'm drilling screws into the back privacy fence, fortifying the cedar planks that had been nailed in by the previous owner. As I drive them, a ruthlessness surges in me, a stubbornness and a resentment – an anger that hasn't yet risen in my writing. I am "hard-ening the target" with these labors, proud that I am doing so, appalled at my previous laxity and trust, doubtful that these measures will provide protection enough. Driving the screws in revenge – each a statement that I will not bow though I have no courage; each an angry wish to be left in peace with the sweet twilights and the luxury of lounging with faith in the night sounds and the city. This is not introspection. I'm contemplating razor wire (how to make it unobtrusive but evident and yet harmless to the cats that scale the fences hourly). I'm beginning to under-stand the portcullis and the rampart, the

64

doughy merchants of the frontier settlement begging for a hero to wear their badge, the tribesmen packing their mud walls high and hard against the barbarians.

I'm driving the screws and setting my jaw, gritting my teeth. I'm determined, inspired in a way writing these notes has not inspired me. Physical. The hands gesturing toward some ample retribution, laboring on a project. I see ways you can still get to me, and how simple it was for you before. I'm learning about my place. I'm not so much put in my place as re-making a place I took for granted. I'm disinviting the predator, calling you to have a second thought, pass by and seek another who is as I was: one who assumes that minding his own business is enough.

· · · · · · · · · ·

Shall we call Don a craven opportunist of suffering, self-indulgent and humorless? Shall we assert that he is simply unwilling to forget a morbid captivity? Certainly those friends who have seen some of these pages thus far have counseled him with a retreating silence about such a likelihood.

Or shall we allow the possibility that he is yet unable to escape a certain concurrence of events, of ordeals and mentalities long in the making, except by a submission to these words, to this sentence, though the escape such a sentence promises is illusory? He has vowed repeatedly to put these words away, and perhaps he will when he understands what that means, and if it is what he means.

Shall we consider it part of his begging?

He believes he seeks a moral stance in the world – an undertaking somewhat limited since he, like many, has assumed it is morally better to extend himself toward the sorrows and sufferings – the vulnerability, such as he knows it – of others, rather than to also seek to understand their joys and pleasures. But who can choose suffering, or joy, in its fullness?

Before Gregory, before the WTC attacks, he could turn his face upward with what seems now a luxurious anxiety and disgust toward the stealth bomber passing low over his house from Central Command, a black tomb tablet called into the air to parade for the Super Bowl festivities at the stadium equally nearby.

He has written his curse letter to anger. He has pledged his love to his wife and his inspiration to his art and his discipline to a mortgage. He has volunteered his days at a runaway shelter. He has written the checks to the causes and admitted, at least to himself, that he has not written as many as he could. He has believed he was raised up engaged with worthy obstacles, most of them close to home.

Now the obstacles, perhaps not so unprecedented as they might seem at present, appear more demanding of him and his neighbors than ever: how to resist the abrupt muteness presumed to pass for citizenship, the conformity equated with patriotism; how to oppose the fear mongers and the inner fear and those who manufacture for the powerful a small, heavily advertised product line of reality, one especially dismissive of human complexity; how to undermine the god-peddlers of martyrdom and heroism; how to diffuse and undo the ventriloquism of hateful virtue and seamless misdirection; how to defy the sentimental servants of an increasingly arrogant state?

Don knows he has been lucky. In his travels with the golden

passport, he has walked unmolested before the guns of a half dozen dictatorships and stood as a bewildered pilgrim at the frozen pond where the ashes of the slaughtered were dumped. He has been robbed discreetly, with expertise, in various picturesque plazas. He has not spoken the language and yet has often been taken to the food, to the medicine, by strangers. And he has played the part one plays in meeting the cosmic quota of near misses at intersections and on moonlit islands, before exploding cans, beneath falling rocks and suspicious moles, in the company of spreading fire and wayward fork lift and supplicating pederast, in the undertow.

He and Lisa have even once discovered their back door – *that door* – left open all night and nothing come of it.

Observe him a few days after Gregory's invasion, driving a rental car since Gregory has stolen his. (Because it is America, one of Don and Lisa's friends who had heard a rumor about the invasion verified it by sighting the rental car in Don and Lisa's driveway. Anyone could see the car was a rental, the slight, cheap white compact no one would aspire to own.) As Don turns into the sunlight, he sees on the windshield the smears of cat tracks that frustrate him every morning, evidence of the nightly marauding of the pride of strays who stow themselves under the house. He is soothed by this insistence from the unchanged.

He hopes his car won't be found, though this would mean more money lost. He wants to imagine that Gregory has taken it out of state on some great flight to a new, more worthy life. He wants this crime to be exotic, meaningful, unique.

Some part of him also hopes his car won't be found because Gregory has had his hands on it. (Or perhaps, Don thinks, Gregory has not dared to remove his gloves to drive? Good.)

Don's car is discovered, however, eight days after the invasion, abandoned not more than five miles from Lisa and Don's house, on North 20th Street and Martin Luther King Boulevard, in College Hill, an impoverished neighborhood that is also home to the community radio station that broadcasts those programs on snitch culture and human rights and the enduring need to question the authorities – programs to which Don attends with bewitched enthusiasm.

On the way to College Hill, Don is relieved: the crime is completed, the act, at last, ended. (This relief fades rapidly, since Gregory has also stolen Don's laptop computer, on which Don kept his writing from the previous ten years, including his journal. Don has copies of all this work, of course, but now, to his disquiet, so does Gregory, or someone else.) Oddly, as he nears College Hill, Don also feels the unease of one preparing to meet an old acquaintance whom he hasn't encountered in many years, or perhaps to view the corpse of a distant relative from childhood.

Don and Lisa find a police officer waiting with the car, a thick, friendly, reassuring Nordic woman in her mid-thirties, eight years assigned to College Hill, and most of that on the night shift. Don's car, she says, has been there no more than a few hours, but someone has already tried, unsuccessfully, to pry open the driver's side door.

Black fingerprint dust and hand smears cover the exterior, with a few perfect, clean squares from which the police lab might glean some decent prints, though there is no guarantee, the officer cautions, that they will turn out to be Gregory's.

"The car could have been traded for drugs," the officer says, "or we might not have this guy's prints on file."

The interior smells at first of pine deodorizer but then less so, closer to actual pine sap on a dampened, fresh-cut log. Except it is not a clean odor – no breeze in it. The smell is of the search for a particular touch amid the vast traffic of generally invisible contact, for some record of identity.

Don slides behind the wheel. The car has been driven approximately four hundred miles since Gregory took it with its nearly full tank of fuel.

Before Don pulls away, the officer defines the term *carjacking* for him. He must appear to need that.

"Don't stop for gas anywhere around here," she counsels, smiling.

Don realizes the seat has been moved from its usual position, pushed all the way back. He drives it home like that, tentative and slightly dazed at an unaccustomed distance from the wheel. He feels as though he is almost inhabiting the body that had been there (imitating it somehow, and by this perhaps teaching himself something about it). Though whose body might that be? And what kind of victim might its owner think it is, if its owner entertains such possibilities? Does it really long to flash money for its friends, as Lisa's stories of Gregory have imagined?

On the floor Don finds a pink admission wristband from the Castle, a nightclub near downtown Tampa, and an unopened condom. Cigarette ashes and trails of spilled soda. On the driver's seat, between his legs, a smear of red lipstick.

. . . .

What are you, if you're nothing to be gotten
over?

If one is watching oneself, what makes one
think that watcher is more worthy than any
other witness, just because that watcher is trying to see both sides of the eye at once?

Shame often comes to me in the night, the

69

shame of being powerless, of being human. I didn't face the moment when I could discover how much courage I might have. The question, unanswered, remains intact. (How valuable would an answer be? How much could one rely on it?)

I told a therapist Lisa and I visit from time to time about my shame (which at that moment seemed too strong a word to describe the embarrassment emanating from even the most banal and minute encounters with friends and strangers).

The therapist asserted that well-adjusted people depend on necessary illusions: that, for instance, they are more well-liked (or more prominent in the minds of others) than they are; that they have more control over their lives than they have.

"You could say that depressed people are more realistic," she suggested.

So what kind of fantasy is adjustment, and how realistic do I wish to be? (If one can choose to be realistic?) In thinking of you – in trying to let you come close enough so that I might see you clearly, now that you are at an apparently lengthening remove – there is an immense, glacial weight, a tentacular slowness that imbues and overtakes me. I'm mortified. Some heavy feathers are brushing my eyelids, and I am aware of something moving more deeply into me, and I must hold up my head because I feel I am curling into a fetal position as I stand.

I can be sipping coffee quietly and the next moment raging about how we "must find these terrorists and get them!" It's the rage of people of all epochs who seem tiresome and irritatingly trapped by an intractable past....

Of course, I'm trying to kill you now, and it's profoundly unsatisfying because I'm not finished with you. I don't know what I will do when I am finished with you. The notion stumps me ... frightens me?

I am afraid of the wearying repetitions of my life just prior to your appearance. Boredom, or the anxiety of its coming – interrupted by you. And now these new repetitions.

• • • • • • • • • •

A friend gives Don and Lisa a personal essay she happened upon in a magazine – an essay, she says, about a home invasion.

The essay, however, is not about that topic, literally or otherwise. It's about a slit in a bedroom screen, a flashlight shined in the eyes. It's about what horrible things happened to other people and didn't happen to the narrator. Don is haughty about the piece, at first, and relieved. The essay writer's encounter was not like his and Lisa's. It was, in fact, "less" than theirs: the intruder didn't even come into the house. So – Don thinks though he does not say it – their experience of Gregory is "safe," preserved from the violation of having been similar to another's experience, secured from that invasion of reality.

Why would anyone want an experience like Don and Lisa's to

remain solely their property? And what is the property in question? The desire to exclude denies the fact – daily supported by the assured, if questionable, production of statistics – that each is one of many, that our experiences are not even wholly our own. In fact, because they occur to others, and have occurred to others, they seem somehow foregone – after the visceral impact has subsided.

What is it, other than the loss of a certain notion of meaning, a certain claim on individuality, that makes one prouder of having survived terror than of, say, getting a promotion at the office?

The insistence that the attacks of 9/11 were wholly unprecedented seems to derive from a similar impulse, fed by an elusive but resilient fear: to mingle our catastrophe with any other is to lose it along with everything else that was lost.

The U.S. leadership appears to have understood this fear as an opportunity – hence its unwillingness to acknowledge the attacks as an especially dreadful episode in a long and lengthening global series of political violence with complex geopolitical and economic causes and difficult solutions. Declaring the attacks unprecedented eventually requires the conclusion that unprecedented reactions are necessary. It also reaffirms the illusion that the irredeemable is un-American, a burden other peoples bear. Thus, an anguished predicament of the personal, the intimate, is terribly simplified and, given the might of the nation in question, presented to the rest of the world as requiring inescapable consequences.

• • • • • • • • • • •

Had Gregory killed Lisa and Don, the act would have been a double violation – because it also would have been a death humiliated by banality. The crime would have been commonplace, as most murders are, and without voice except for the official record and the newspaper, the local gossip, and the slivers of imagery or detail glinting in the memory of those who heard about it. In this regard, Don sometimes thinks of a book of murder scene photos from early twentieth century New York he saw years before Gregory. The horror of the scenes is often aestheticized by the distance in time – the killing seems weirdly quaint. And the subject in each photo has become his or her death only.

Yet whose death is it now?

Lisa says she loves her house but it is now also a trap, a problem whose terms change with the hour or the abrupt foregrounding of various furnishings. Of course, it is the Gregory now in her that she is fleeing as she is planning to flee. It is the Gregory that makes her aware, that way. Don doesn't think this situation would please Gregory, necessarily. Gregory didn't want that – did he?

• • • • • • • • • • •

Do you lie sometimes, nearly catatonic,
cracked-out on the couch in one of the projects that the city painted pink and, when it
faded into years, bright blue to highlight the
poverty, to humiliate and warn? Does your
sister try to rouse you, wondering if you're
overdosing? Or does she welcome you slipping away? Or does she ignore you, sitting

down beside you and turning on the TV, opening a box of pizza? Or is that young woman your girlfriend? Your wife? Your brother's wife? Or just another who sleeps here tonight and maybe tomorrow night, a nobody in a stranger's place, like you?

Are there gold chains on your chest?

Is that a great light from the Castle in your wide pupils?

I come across a line in a book of aphorisms: "The voice is a second face." It's your only face, even though we get a surprise call from our former neighbor, a city councilman, who assures us that the police are closing in on a gang they've had under surveillance. He's probably running for mayor.

The government is talking of the need for secret military tribunals. It won't release the names of hundreds who've been arrested and yet not charged with anything. To that, you'd probably say: You think that's new?

Or maybe you are a teacher's son.

Who do you fear in the night? In the day? What gets *your* curse letter?

Once, in my twenties, my girlfriend at the time and I got on the subway somewhere in lower Manhattan. It was late and the only other passenger was a man bearing a white cane, seated at the far end of the car. As soon as the train started, he jumped up and came toward us, muttering to himself and then railing, as he beat his cane against the seats. I remember being very calm as he approached, studying the hand that didn't hold the cane, watchful for a weapon. The man seemed to grow even more furious. He shouted and slapped that cane all around our legs, our arms, our heads, never touching us, as he passed and stumbled into the next car. All around us, mad and meticulous.

. . . .

Among the circle of items on the desk in Don's study – half a vole jaw; a silvery, rumpled patch of lichen; a Chinese chop bearing an approximation of Don's name in Mandarin; a sealed syringe bottle full of charms from the witches' market in La Paz; a crumbling leather coin purse containing a gold quarter dollar dated 1874 – among these items present on the day Don tore through his wallet for Gregory, there has accumulated a stack of newspaper articles about the Zantops and two slivers of back door glass.

Now Don adds a disposable camera. He has seen the man whom Lisa thinks might be Gregory pass several more times, heading to and from the grocery store at the end of the street. By chance in his car, he has seen the man apparently enter the green apartment house on Platt Avenue, two blocks in the other direction. On several occasions he has tried to sneak a photograph of the man but has failed to find a camera in time. Now he knows where it is.

Soon, at evening, the man strides past the house again, bound, presumably, for the grocery store, and Don, brushed by an awareness of absurdity, pauses at the window. He then rushes for the camera, but when he returns, the man has vanished. He decides that now is the moment to look more closely at the man and resolve everything. He gets in his car and drives toward the grocery store, as though he were merely going for milk and bread but hoping to pass the man, perhaps within only a few feet. He coasts the four blocks to the store, eager to be casual, wanting to convince himself that he is not engaged as he is, glancing down each side street he passes, not finding the man and not wanting to turn around. At the end of the fourth block, across from the grocery store, he decides the man must already have crossed the broad parking lot and gone into the store. He parks and enters the bright, white cavern, shoving his gait forward, his eyes.

Twice he marches along both ends of the aisles, peering down each, as though searching for clues to the location of an obscure and puzzling product, deciding that when he spots the man, he will pass close by him to discover if this person will reveal himself, through some slip of recognition, to be Gregory. He decides that he will even take the chance, should it arise, to utter "Excuse me" as he reaches for an item and perhaps extract a reply from the man, a test of the voice.

He finally comes to rest among banks of gleaming plastic soda bottles, with the thoughtful gaze of the thoughtless, of one who has forgotten what he has come for and is unwilling to give up, of one who was almost certain and yearns to be certain again.

A woman in a straw hat appears, and though she seems not to take special notice of him as she passes and pulls bottles from the shelves and settles them into her shopping cart, he feels the brightness of the room, the high ceilings, the packages stupidly there, himself a stranger.

In what seems to him later a silly, broad gesture, he turns his head as though he has just remembered something vital and must attend to it immediately. He marches out of the store and never mentions it to Lisa.

. . . .

Just after the police had finished their report and left the house, I went to the pharmacy photo counter two blocks from our house to buy film to record the scene for the insurance, in case they needed such documentation. I also wanted pictures to make vivid what had happened (though I've only shown them to two or three friends). I stood shaking in line, behind three women at the counter sorting through snapshots, deciding which to keep. Fully mundane. And I understood what it was to be alone and marked only to myself, with a knowledge like a radiance no one else could detect. I remembered women I've known who had been raped, and I began faintly, ever so faintly, to perceive the radiance that trespass bestowed on them.

Of course, I wanted to shout to those women at the counter: "Don't you know what's just happened to me?"

But it was happening again right at that moment, near or far, to someone else. Maybe it had happened to them not so long ago, and it was far worse. What was the subject of their pictures?

Everything about the store and the motions

of the ordinary seemed a great betrayal to my fresh understanding of affliction. An affront to suffering – as all ordinary, clean, orderly, and hopeful life appears to be. As my life has often been.

Everything that spoke of order and convenience – the signs and the ads – all of it was invoking the darts of small irony, calling them out to pierce me and make me smile the broken jug smile. There was the shadowy underside of the happy mask, rigid and distorting. There was the other side of all light and order, the place where the hall in the mirror turns and vanishes but somehow remains, leading away and unreachable. There was the other side of each bright object and each clear label, the sticky side that affixes itself to the familiar and available surfaces, the reclusive surfaces of things, which cannot be touched easily.

I stood there with those women whom I would never know nor who would ever know me, only sharing that moment in time, most of us unaware that we were sharing it, that we were together in that present – or presence – and we were sorting images, deciding which we could keep, wondering what went wrong, trying to understand our intentions. Or we were buying the means to capture some images not in our minds, or not the same as in our minds.

Had I never been alone like that before? In

the days after you, the aloneness was like a
thick, seamless solution through which I la-
bored merely to walk.

At the photo counter, I was disheveled, just
dressed, oily, unshaven. What did the look
on my face say? What could it say? None of us
knows out of what epiphany the person beside us has just fallen.

• • • • • • • • • •

On a day in early spring 2002, a student in Don's nonfiction writing workshop and a member of ROTC – let's call him Jack – claims
he wants to write about a close friend from his platoon who was
recently killed in Afghanistan. Jack's friend was part of a helicop-
ter crew of approximately twenty soldiers on night reconnais-
sance in the mountains. Hugging the terrain, they had flown low
over a summit and were surprised by ground fire. Their ship was
hit, and the impact caused one of the crew, who should have
been wearing a safety line, to fall out. They circled back and re-
trieved this fallen crewman, but in the melee, he fell out again,
was captured and executed on the spot by the enemy. Trying to
rescue the soldier a second time, the chopper was hit so hard the
crew was forced to ditch. There ensued a nine-hour battle with
more than three hundred Taliban fighters, who, according to the
intelligence given the chopper crew before their mission, were
not supposed to be there. Jack's friend survived four hours. But
while running with his machine gun, his elbows held high because he was so muscular, Jack reckoned, he was shot through
the side and the heart.

To help Jack try to focus his perceptions, Don has invited him
to his office to tape himself as he talks about snapshots taken by

his friend in Afghanistan, which the friend had sent to family and which arrived three days after his death. There is nothing unusual about these images of infantry tents in the desert, soldiers posing with weapons, the ritual of one of the guys in the outfit being given a pink belly by the group on his birthday. But they are not ordinary to Jack, who explains each to Don, unable to settle on a beginning or an ending, his monologue threaded with obscure military terms and acronyms he assumes anyone would understand. His tone is sometimes choked, sometimes profane, infatuated with the textbook explanation of how a piece of equipment works or what a certain kind of training entails; and sometimes it is worried and world-weary, though he is only twenty-two and has been in the service three years. Had he not gone into ROTC and come to college, were he not here seeking Don's help with his writing, he would have been with his friend and the rest of their unit, perhaps even on this mission.

"I don't have the whole story," he admits to Don. "I haven't seen the videotape of the firefight, you know, from the unmanned aircraft. They had it orbiting the scene during the entire nine-hour duration. They've got the tape down at MacDill. A special operations office has it. I don't know when I'll be able to see it, if I'll ever be able to see it.

"The enemy doesn't have night vision capability, so they were basically shooting blind. We've got infrared laser sights and night vision goggles, and that's the only thing that kept our guys in the fight for so long. That, and we train so much about controlling the rates of fire. The minimum combat load is 210 rounds, which is seven magazines, and I'm sure they went in with a lot more than that. But to make it last nine hours is incredible, especially when I myself have downloaded ten magazines in a matter of moments on missions before."

Jack's friend had been a math teacher before joining the service. Like Jack, he was third-generation infantry. He was thirty years old. Already the facts of his life and death, such as Jack is aware of them, are fanning out and intermingling with the facts of Jack's own life, taking on multiple identities, shifting allegiances to the knowable.

Jack continues to explain the photographs, needing to be heard but not hearing himself, perhaps never to hear.

Experience isn't valuable, Don had told Jack's class, just because it occurs to you.

As though Don comprehended precisely the nature of this curious composite – experience.

A student in that class had replied: "It's like you're writing a story you just happen to be in."

On the tape, which Jack forgot to take with him from Don's office – purposely, Don realized later – Jack says, flatly, "I'm sure there was a large exit wound."

Jack's friend left money for the unit here in the States to have a round of Guinness, his favorite drink, in his memory, which the unit did.

"I start each drinking night with a Guinness, in honor of him," Jack says at the end of the tape. "I hate the taste of the stuff."

. . . .

Later that day, Don attends a meeting with a consultant imported from New York City to advise faculty on student writing and critical thinking. The consultant is soon aware that most of those present are well-versed in the techniques he has been hired to offer, so he opens the discussion to all, and the hour is managed with goodwill and unexpected enthusiasm.

At the end of the session, he asks everyone's pardon to read a two-page essay by his sixteen-year-old son about the World Trade Center attacks. The prose is a model of reason – calling for a deeper understanding of the hijackers' motives, for thought rather than action for action's sake. It soon becomes evident the piece is less an object of paternal pride than the man's magical spell against terror and madness, a desperate hope for his son and for us all.

As the reading proceeds, Don thinks of the local teenager who killed himself recently by flying a single-engine Cessna into the twentieth floor of the Bank of America building across from the university. Though some offices were ruined, no one else was hurt in this piteous and farcical instance of personal expression. The boy left a note declaring his sympathy with bin Laden, but the authorities were eager to assert that he had no ties to terrorist organizations, perhaps more so since he had flown over MacDill before turning toward downtown and, according to the outraged local press, had met no resistance because all the fighter planes usually stationed at the base were on assignment elsewhere.

The consultant concludes his reading and declares, "This is the kind of thinking we hope to instill in our students."

Eager to comfort him, a lifelong New Yorker, and perhaps to comfort ourselves, everybody agrees, and the consultant, rising quickly to shake hands and move on to the wine and cheese reception, blinks away tears.

• • • • • • • • • • •

While Lisa and Don work in the front yard, the man Lisa thinks might be Gregory if she could only hear him speak, the man Don followed to the grocery store, saunters down the street toward them. He is huge, vertical and vastly muscular in a tank top, rakish with the pirate bandana. His arms bow outward from his sides as though he wears a pair of six-guns and, nearing the climax of a cartoon showdown, is about to draw.

"Here's your chance," Don says to her.

A few hundred feet away, the man encounters another young man walking a poodle – someone he knows well enough to stop and chat with for a moment before moving on. He tosses a couple of final comments about a Florida–Florida State football game over his shoulder to the poodle man as he passes Don and Lisa.

"How you doin', y'all?" he says to Don.

After he is out of earshot, Lisa concludes, seemingly relieved, "No, that's not him. The voice. And the planes of his face, too sharp-featured."

Don had studied him in a somewhat friendly way from behind sunglasses. He imagines, however, that this attitude somehow unsettled the man, though the man rippled so majestically in the spring sunshine it seemed he and his body could only have fallen from a great height of possible destiny and must surely be wasted by living this way, walking to and from the grocery store. It wasn't a body that should be walking, anywhere.

· · · · · · · · · · ·

"Now I have to tie you up," Gregory said in the dimness of the bathroom.

The distance between them all, it seemed, was at last coming to an end. The terror surged back into Don, as a soft collapse between his shoulder blades.

Then Gregory asked if Don and Lisa had anything with which he could bind them.

This unexpected request later seemed to them his first faltering. It conjured a peculiar pause during which Lisa noticed the belt of her bathrobe, hanging on the door behind Gregory, and Don tried not look at the cord of the hair dryer beside their intruder. Objects on all sides of him, of them – potential transformations, possible fates.

"We won't go anywhere," Lisa pleaded with Gregory.

"You'll go out the window if I don't tie you up."

"No," she said. "We couldn't even identify your face. We don't have our glasses on."

He hesitated. Perhaps this statement saved them? Perhaps Don having called out "9-1-1" as Gregory came forth had created a limit to his intention? Only a few minutes had elapsed, but now each one rounded into its fullness with a peculiar heft and agitation.

"You got any jewelry, gold . . . stuff like that?"

"We're teachers," Lisa said, almost scoffing.

"Which one's tinted?" he demanded, holding up Don's keys.

"What?" they said.

"The cars. Which is tinted, the windows?"

"Neither," Don said. He still wonders if this exchange, too, might have been some little test. Surely Gregory knew beforehand that there were two cars. He surely knew neither had a fully tinted windshield. Don's keys hung on a ring attached to a tab of hand-tooled leather on which a goose lifting from a piney pond was depicted. Don had purchased it two years before at the prison gift shop at the state penitentiary near Marquette, Michigan. He'd stopped there while bicycling along Lake Superior, spurred by a vacationer's curiosity and the impulse of self-caressing irony. For a while he had kept the price tag, which carried the number of the inmate who had made the leather tab, because he had hoped to write a poem about it.

84

. . . .

A soap bubble floats on the water in the kitchen sink.

Actually, it floats on a space it puts between itself and the water, always – so says one of my colleagues at the university, a chemist.

What makes the molecules of soap cling most ferociously to each other, so that they cling even when they are pressured to stretch and thus make a bubble? What compels them to insist on that space between themselves and the molecules of water?

What's the distance that's kept from us? What's the distance that keeps us?

. . . .

Don has decided that, if he cannot yet throw out the newspaper articles on his desk (articles about the Zantops and about 9/11), he must put them away. This is more than a start and less than a finish. Of what, he is uncertain. As he places the stack in a cardboard box, he begins to reread the article on the top, from the April 5, 2002, *Valley News*.

State's Case Detailed an Anatomy of Two Murders

Hanover NH

Just before the two teenagers knocked on the door at 115 Trescott Road in Etna, they made another of the many missteps that would mark their bumbling but determined journey toward murder. They left behind in their car a tape recorder that was supposed to bolster their ruse of conducting an "environmental survey."

But would-be killers Robert Tulloch and James Parker had evil luck that day. The door they'd chosen at random was answered by Half Zantop, a trusting and helpful professor of earth sciences at Dartmouth College – who knew The Mountain School.

According to a lengthy and detailed statement offered in court yesterday by Kelly Ayotte, the head of the homicide division of the New Hampshire Attorney General's office, the teenagers falsely told Zantop they were students at "The Mountain School," an elite private school in Vershire, near their homes in Chelsea. The school is a working farm where high school juniors spend four months at a time studying academics and learning about sustainable rural living.

"I like what The Mountain School does. I like the programs at The Mountain School," Half Zantop told the boys. He let them in, ushered them into the study, set up chairs for them, and for more than 10 minutes, patiently answered Tulloch's questions while Parker took sham notes.

When the phony interview was over, Zantop offered the boys some constructive criticism: Be more prepared next time. He said he knew someone in their area who could help them with their survey, and he sought the number in the phone book. Not finding it there, he took out his wallet, allowing the boys a glimpse of a large wad of cash.

While the victim's attention was diverted, Tulloch reached into a backpack containing the tools the had assembled: duct tape, plastic "zip ties" that could be used as handcuffs, and two $100 military knives.

Pulling out one of the foot-long knives, Tulloch leaped on Half Zantop. Susanne Zantop, who was preparing lunch in the kitchen, heard her husband scream.

By Ayotte's account the brutal murders of Half and Susanne Zantop on Jan. 27, 2001, began growing months earlier from the most mundane of seeds: adolescent ennui. Tulloch and Parker were "bored" with their small, rural hometown, where they attended public Chelsea School.

In early 2000, when Tulloch was 16 and Parker 15, the two friends decided they would make their own adventure and go to Australia. Investigators would later seize notes of the careful calculations by which they arrived at the sum they would need for the trip: $10,000.

Ayotte said the idea to raise that money by illegal means came from Tulloch. Her descriptions of the murderous arc the two teenagers followed is based largely on the four or five interviews Parker gave to prosecutors after his arrest, after reaching an agreement to plead guilty to being an accomplice to second-degree murder in exchange for a recommended sentence of 25 years to life. In that account, every bad idea the boys nurtured as they became more and more consumed with their plotting came from Tulloch: stealing cars to raise the money, "jumping" people to rob them of their ATM cards and PIN numbers, killing their robbery victims so there would be no witnesses – even killing a police officer if necessary to avoid arrest.

... Tulloch did not contest Ayotte's version of events when given the chance in court.

The boys' preparations for that escalation were painstaking. They scouted out a house on Goose Green Road in Vershire, dug a grave for their intended victim at an abandoned house nearby, gathered knives and duct tape and zip ties. On July 19, 2000, they dressed in black, waited till night, and then cut the phone line to the house. Their plan: While Parker hid in the bushes at the side of the house, Tulloch would tell a story about their car having broken down, and ask to use the phone.

To their surprise the homeowner came to the door with a gun in his hand – which he showed to Tulloch while rebuffing his request to come in.

The boys were discouraged by the failure, and Parker was scared, but neither was deterred. They went back to stealing mail until frustration once again focused their attention on robbery. This time, they decided to use stun guns to keep their victims from fighting back. That plan suffered a temporary setback when Tulloch's mother intercepted and returned their first mail-order purchase of stun guns, but the boys succeeded in secretly purchasing another set. They bought bigger knives over the Internet, and then went to a military surplus store in Barre VT to accessorize the sheaths with custom straps and clips. They began reconnoitering homes in Rochester VT, sometimes using binoculars.

The boys considered waiting at darkened houses and ambushing the residents as they returned home, but settled instead on a ruse to get inside: They would claim to be conducting an environmental survey. On January 19, 2001, they tried to execute that plan at a home on North Hollow Road in Rochester VT, but the homeowner turned them away, saying he was busy tarring his indoor pool.

Within the next day or so, the boys turned their sights to Hanover, where they knew a lot of wealthy people lived. They drove across the Connecticut River. They parked at a home on Trescott Road near the Zantops' house. Their SOG Seal 2000 knives were strapped to their legs. But their nerve apparently failed them. After charging up the driveway of the unidentified home, the boys "decided not to go forward with their plan that day," Ayotte said.

Another attempt in the same neighborhood a week or so later also failed, when no one answered the boys' knocks. More determined now to find someone to kill, they simply moved on to the next house: the Zantops'.

Half Zantop struggled wildly as Tulloch stabbed him repeatedly in the chest and slashed his face. A card table was knocked over and papers went flying, Half was screaming terribly, which brought Susanne running from the kitchen. She screamed and grabbed for her husband to help him. But Parker, who had also pulled a knife from the backpack, seized her and held her.

Tulloch stopped stabbing Half and looked at Parker. "Slit her throat," he said.

Parker did and let Susanne fall. Tulloch slit Half's throat and then stabbed Susanne repeatedly.

In a rush, the boys grabbed Half's wallet and ran from the home, leaving behind a fingerprint and a bloody boot print. After driving to a remote road to wash their hands and knives in the snow, they suddenly realized that had left behind the sheaths to the knives. . . .

In a bizarre twist, one of the boys' first moves in the hours after the murders was to head to Burlington, where they visited a bookstore and looked at books on killing, including one about how soldiers deal with the issue. They eventually decided to return to Hanover to try to recover the sheaths, but it was too late: a friend of the Zantops had discovered the crime, and there was a police officer standing in the driveway when they drove past. . . .

Three days later, with the region buzzing over their shocking crime, the boys set out for Colorado with the $340 from Half's wallet. The night before he left, Tulloch told his girlfriend, Christiana Usenza, that he had done something bad, and the wound on his leg was from a knife – not from running against a maple sap spigot in the woods, as he had told friends at school. He had cut himself during the murders.

The boys aborted their trip and returned home when Tulloch's wound became too painful. As time passed and police released no details of the crime, they began to believe they had gotten away with it, that they were "all set."

That illusion was soon smashed. Investigators traced the sheaths to the manufacturers of the knives, then found records of the sale of two such knives to Parker. The boys fled again after being questioned by investigators, on February 15, 2001, but only got as far as Indiana before being picked up at a truck stop.

"It's a house of cards," Ayotte quoted Tulloch as telling the officer who arrested him. "It took me 17 years to build, and I just blew it up. I can't put it back up again."

Tulloch was sentenced to life in prison without parole, Parker to a minimum of twenty-five years. What will their relations be with their victims at age forty-five, say, or seventy-one? And each with his cell, his mirror?

On the day of their separate sentencings, Parker wept and apologized to the Zantops' two daughters, but Tulloch, according to the press, "kept a blank, inscrutable expression," as he was "berated" by one of the daughters, who concluded, "Rather than focus on the inhumanity and monstrosity – and sheer stupidity – of their brutal and senseless deaths, I console myself by trying to perpetuate the essence of my parents."

Don lets himself wonder, but only for a moment, what the life expectancy in prison might be. He places this last newspaper article into the cardboard box and seals it with tape – a ritual of improvised, intimate necessity, but also, he would admit, a barbaric luxury and, to the ripening pain of the truly injured, surely an affront.

• • • • • • • • • •

Once, I tried to use you – the story of you – on a
woman at the auto dealership where I had
purchased my car. I needed information about
that purchase for my insurance on a matter

90

unrelated to you, but I'd misplaced my records from years before. I asked her if she would look it up – a major inconvenience to her, carrying no apparent reward. She was rigidly silent, so I mentioned that you had broken in and stolen my car, etc.

"I'm sorry to hear that," she said, politely rebuffing me with no offer of help.

Of course I deserved her disinterest. I must have sounded as phony as you claiming to be homeless.

That woman had been minding her own business, she thought, and there I was, lying.

At times, now more than a year after you, I'm expecting suddenness, and this curbs my capacity for simple pleasure. I sometimes say aloud – as if to remind myself of a crucial forgotten fact that might fortify me instead of giving me night terrors that throw me sometimes like an ink stain against the bed sheets – "the angel of death swept a wing over me." How do you like that melodramatic role? It doesn't really help. In those moments, I don't see the proverbial glass as half empty so much as I am trying to anticipate it being shattered.

I feel dishonest, overwhelmingly so, and not just because of that episode at the auto dealership. We appear so little in time. We know hardly anything of the time before our birth, nothing of the time after our death. And what of the time of our living – what of that?

Had your coming to Lisa and me been a lone, sensational event in, say, an otherwise remote, peasant life – you might have been singularly memorable. But because you appeared amid the daily media pilgrimage of people far away and right here burdened by their extravagant misfortunes, you are a constant reminder that things are "bad out there" beyond our clean, quiet rooms, and we should be able to take some action to break the moral locked-in syndrome that seems to be what witnessing the world has become for those of us not struggling just to survive. Of course, Out There is also In Here, and always has been, and always could be; and we don't know what to do, except turn away not so much to rescue ourselves as to save some capacity for life – which, it is true, might finally just be transformed into the pursuit of more purchasing power or some new protectionist spectatorship.

I can imagine what you'd say to this: Shut up and be glad, you don't know the first thing about your own neighbors.

And what do you know? What do you know?

· · · · · · · · · · ·

On May 30, 2002, the search operation at the World Trade Center is officially brought to a close. The final girder is ceremoniously drawn from the pit. No speeches or sermons are delivered. The *Times* reports that "more than 19,000 body parts have been recovered but 1,800 victims have yet to be identified."

A few days before, the *Times* republished a photograph of trapped people peering from the upper windows of one of the towers before it collapsed, an image withdrawn from the media sphere in America almost immediately after the attacks, perhaps because it was unbearable in what it made so vivid about each soul's status amid the way of things. In the photograph, some people are clinging to the outside of the structure. Some of these jumped to avoid the flames closing in on them. Some were forced to let go. All perished. Most of us know the image now. But no one knows those minutes – only the minutes that image inspired, only that invasion.

On his back deck redolent with orange blossoms, Don broods on his psychologist-relation telling him that she has worked with several trauma patients who, in addition to the usual struggles of mending, find themselves jealous of the public validation that accompanied the suffering and death on 9/11.

"At least somebody had acknowledged that it happened," she observed.

Don thinks of all the deadly seekers of paradise – whether it be the afterlife land of seventy virgins or some equally sentimental Australia, or simply the dubious paradise of becoming visible by whatever means. He thinks of W. H. Auden's poem, "September 1, 1939," which was read often on the radio in the days after the attacks, to console and inspire. He recalls that Auden believed one of the poem's most famous lines, "we must love one another or die," was untrue, and later in life he revised it to read, "we must love one another and die." The earlier version, however, prevails in anthologies and classrooms.

Soon after the attacks, there were already reports of bootleg videos sold in the street markets of China in which footage of the actual conflagration was intercut with footage from Hollywood films – but without the preciousness of a caveat to this effect. Don tries to imagine the day when most people won't already know beforehand any of the details of the 9/11 catastrophe, when the events of that day and the changes it conferred on lives around the globe will be compressed into a phrase like "the rape of Nanking" or the "the conquest of Gaul," and it begins to join the faded murders and the myriad, vital distinctions sweeping into the vortex of the great smallness drawing toward eternity.

Horrible passage. Horrible work of busyness. Every second an anniversary of the lost.

The blade-beat of a police chopper draws him back to the evening around him. It circles on the north horizon – over College Hill, he guesses, perhaps area 84 on the crime grid – and then heads toward his part of town. Its searchlight is like the barbed finger of a lesser god who would, if he could, flip the tops off houses to get at the truth there.

. . . .

It's August, 2002. A radio talk show featured a priest who's just published a book about his first-hand experience of the WTC attacks: aiding the injured and then attempting to comfort those questioning why God would allow such suffering.

He said he eventually found himself asking things like: Did those who jumped from the burning towers commit the sin of suicide?

He sounded so young, this priest. His circular reassurances about the cosmic order seemed drawn from class notes at the seminary – ex-

pressed with the clumsy grasp of one who will
manage to pass the exam but for whom the ven-
erable main points and their pitfalls are still terribly new, still mostly sequestered from the rest
of reality as he has known it, and mostly alien
from each other.

I hope he actually is young.

But he's seen a lot more than I have, no
doubt. And maybe he's comforted some people.
So what's the point in shaking my head at him,
at how his voice made me feel abruptly, perhaps
unjustifiably, older . . . older now than a priest?

Three weeks ago, Lisa and I drove past the
Zantop place on Trescott Road. Yes, that sort of
travel. Past the orange daylilies there extending
themselves like hands to the sun. According to
the newspapers, the house had been put on the
market months ago. No doubt it's been sold.

Though Lisa consented to this mortifying
tour, she'd asked me quite a while ago not to
read any more of this writing to her. She was
being kind.

I don't know what else I'd hoped to discover
in those few minutes going first one way on
Trescott Road and then the other – aside from
the blank assertion that I have no business
there.

This morning, she begged me, wisely, to put
this notebook away for twenty or thirty years,
and go with her to the shore.

"There isn't any word that will finish all

this off," she said. "Who knows? Maybe it has to be somebody else's."

So. There must be an end. Of course. This form demands it – boundaries we can endure or try to violate or gratefully despise, boundaries that assign us clear rights to feelings and situations. And also some composure, since the spirit – my spirit, anyway – possesses so little of its own.

Somebody else will have to show you mercy by shooting you in the knee. This is my last entry. This is the last of my curse letter to you, too, whatever the night brings of fear and rage, whatever's next. This is the last of you. There. I'm not coming back.

∙ ∙ ∙ ∙ ∙ ∙ ∙ ∙ ∙ ∙

Eight months later, a U.S. invasion of Iraq concludes as Iraqi troops surrender or disperse, and military conflict ceases. A statue of the tyrant Saddam Hussein – whose whereabouts are unknown – is pulled down for the television cameras in Baghdad. Various Iraqi groups soon call for the United States to withdraw, but the occupation proceeds apace in the name of bringing democracy to the country. No weapons of mass destruction are yet found – though the president and his associates have insisted for months that their existence posed a threat to the United States and its interests.

"They had to come up with some new justification," one of Don's friends opined at the onset of the offensive. "They were wearing out the dead at the twin towers as a pretext for doing whatever they want."

In general, however, most people Don encounters appear untroubled about the government's fabrications, or about the currently groundless assertion, repeated diligently by the authorities, that evidence exists linking Hussein to the attacks on the World Trade Center. Apparently, the lies are part of a mutual understanding, perhaps part of that "ancient adaptive principle."

Kneeling in his front yard on Sunday evening, Don plants blue daze, as he has for the past several months, brooding.

"Hello," a voice says, and he looks up to find a young woman of vaguely Middle Eastern appearance smiling at him. With an accent springing from somewhere in the upper Midwest, she adds, "They tried to sell me a unit two streets over, but when I saw how beautiful your yard was I told them, 'No, I'll take the one across from *that* house.'"

Now the resident with the greatest seniority on the block, Don thanks her for the compliment and welcomes her. She's a software engineer. It's a "dream job," she says, though it requires her to travel extensively during the week. She motions toward her suitcase on the far curb, awaiting the taxi.

"It seems like a pretty quiet neighborhood," she says, and Don agrees, wondering what that might actually be. He thinks of the peace demonstrations he and Lisa have joined recently – at the gates of MacDill before the invasion of Iraq, and then along nearby Bayshore Boulevard after the war began, with Air Force One swinging past their placards as it landed at Central Command so the president could address troops there. He thinks of having shouted with the other protestors, "No blood for oil!" and one onlooker shouting back, "I hope a dirty bomb kills your kids!" And the sheriff deputies scanning the scene with video cameras. And in the passing traffic, drivers – mostly white men at the wheels of pickups and heavy vehicles – giving the finger to the crowd; and about the same number of drivers offering the peace sign. And one woman shoving her hand up through her yawning sun roof and wagging her index finger as though the protesters were misbehaving children. But most drivers trying not to notice anything at all, their postures stiffening as they passed.

Don wonders what the Zantops might tell the software engineer about the quietness of the neighborhood, and of the global neighborhood, those two who became citizens here so they could vote.

Or Tulloch, what might he say, former president of his high school student council?

As the taxi arrives and Don waves goodbye, he wonders what might be added to the understanding of suddenness.

· · · · · · · · · · ·

"I need an hour," Gregory said, finally, without conviction. "If you don't give it, I'll know, and I'll send my homies for you."

"We won't call the police," Lisa pleaded, "really."

He backed out of the bathroom, closing the door behind him.

Certainly, he had gone to the kitchen for a knife, Don thought.

So why didn't Don and Lisa block the door, then, as they could have easily done, since it opened inward?

They *must* have believed again – as some people are always willing to believe – that at last they were going to be spared, they were going to be safe.

They heard Gregory drag the chair from Don's study and prop it against the bathroom door. More footsteps, back and forth through the house.

Then a distant door slamming. The skid of tires in the driveway.

Then silence, the neighbor children having gone in, presumably, for a snack or a nap.

Here they are, a man and a woman, crouching naked with the anticlimax that makes way for further life – incommensurable, unfixable being. They peer through the dimness at the closed door before them. They listen for a moment to the silence, the future. Ask them if there is no more trusted place, no more fortunate world, as they dare to open the door and creep forth.

Notes

page 6 *"Half Zantop had defensive wounds"*: Douglas Belkin and Stephen
        Kurkjian, "Motive Still Missing in Dartmouth Murder Case,"
        Boston Globe, April 14, 2001.

13 *But the Canadian Centre*: Melanie Kowalski, "Home Invasions,"
    Bulletin of the Canadian Centre for Justice Statistics, June 2002.

13 *443 burglaries*: Tampa Police Department Crime Statistics,
    http://www.tampagov.net/dept_police/Files/Crime_Stats/
    feb2001%20pt1.pdf.

13 *report on home invasions*: James T. Hurley, "Violent Crime Hits
    Home: Home Invasion Robbery," Support Services Bureau, Fort
    Lauderdale Police Department, http://ci.ftlaud.fl.us/police/
    hurley/html.

16 *"Home invaders usually target"*: Hurley, "Violent Crime Hits Home."

20 *"Victims Committed to Social Issues"*: Jodie Tillman, "Victims Com-
    mitted to Social Issues," *Valley News (White River Junction VT)*,
    January 30, 2001.

33 *"most likely exploded"*: Bob Hookway, "Profiler: Killer Acted in An-
    ger," *Valley News*, February 9, 2001.

50 *"This was a crime"*: Harry R. Weber, "New Indictment Raises New
    Questions," *Valley News*, February 24, 2002.

50 *"The only way we will truly know"*: Weber, "New Indictment."

85 *"State's Case Detailed"*: Dan Billin, "State's Case Detailed an Anato-
    my of Two Murders," *Valley News*, April 5, 2002.

Acknowledgments

Thanks to Kathleen and Mike Ochshorn for providing haven in the midst of acute suddenness; to Mary Jane Schenck, whose timely aid helped in the mending of a ruined house; to the Dana Foundation for a summer grant that gave me the opportunity to concentrate on the writing.

Thanks also to Lisa Birnbaum, Richard Chess, Debbie Frederick, Ricardo Hofer, Harriet Lerner, James Lerner, Phil Quinn, John Struss, Stan Rice, and Jeanne Vince, for lending their encouragement and/ or expertise.

And special thanks to Joe Mackall and Dan Lehman, editors, for believing in this book.